Parent Group Counseling

Parent Group Counseling

*A Counselor's Handbook
and Practical Guide*

Frieda A. Lang, Ed.D.

Lexington Books

D.C. Heath and Company/Lexington, Massachusetts/Toronto

Library of Congress Cataloging-in-Publication Data

Lang, Frieda A.
Parent group counseling.

1. Parents—Counseling of—United States.
2. Parenting—Study and teaching—United States.
3. Child rearing—Study and teaching—United States.
4. Group counseling. I. Title.
HQ755.7.L36 1988   649'.1'07   88-7243
    ISBN 0-669-18015-7 (pbk.: alk. paper)

Published simultaneously in Canada
Printed in the United States of America
International Standard Book Number: 0-669-18015-7
Library of Congress Catalog Card Number: 88-7243

The paper used in this publication meets the minimum requirements of
American National Standard for Information Sciences—Permanence of
Paper for Printed Library Materials,
ANSI Z39.48-1984. ∞™

ISBN 0-669-18015-7

88 89 90 91 92 8 7 6 5 4 3 2 1

To all the parents who tried to understand
and learn to cope with the intricacies
of their children's growth and development,
and who taught me as much as I taught them!

Contents

Preface

Self-reliant cooperative human beings are found to grow in stable, trusting homes in which both parents are actively supportive and encouraging, in which discipline is by guidance and example and not by precept or punishment, homes from which the children are encouraged to go forth and to which they are welcome to return. Conversely, disturbed and difficult children come from disturbed and difficult homes, in which care has been insensitive and discipline inappropriate, in which they have been in some degree neglected, or rejected, or subjected to punitive threats, often of abandonment.

—John Bowlby, M.D.
New York Times, 2 March 1974

This guidebook is intended for counselors, psychologists, social workers, and other professionals who wish to assist concerned parents whose children are experiencing some difficulties in various aspects of development. It is based on certain well-established premises.

● The family is the basic and most important unit of society.

● The psychological well-being of the family determines the function and well-being of society in general, and of its children in particular.

● Parents influence the physical, emotional, social, and cognitive growth of their children, and they are the key figures in developing their children's personalities and self-esteem.

Since the 1950s, an overwhelming body of research has revealed that the quality of interpersonal relationships between parents and children significantly affects the developing personality and self-esteem of the child. Furthermore, this research indicates that an ideal environment should provide nurturance and unqualified acceptance of children; show joy and pleasure in their being; and be generous with praise, but provide discipline, consistent limits, guidelines, security, and support. These conditions usually produce a child who is loving, emotionally secure, responsible, intellectually capable, socially adept, and generally a productive member of society. Families in which there is a minimum amount of affection and concern usually produce children who are listless, apathetic, unhappy, have learning problems, and exhibit various adjustment and developmental difficulties. Usually these symptoms surface early and are quite evident when the child enters school.

Psychologists and school counselors have long been aware of these children and the problems they present, and have tried various strategies to improve the child's functioning. In most cases, after conferring with parents, they have counseled only with the child. The fact that this approach has been minimally effective does not reflect on the skill of the counselors or the quality of their involvement. Rather, counselors have failed to deal with the basic cause of the child's malfunctioning—namely the family. Research affirms that only when the child's parents are involved—when they are helped to understand and improve the interpersonal dynamics of the parent–child relationship—is any real improvement noted in the child.

Counseling children on a one-to-one basis, however, is time consuming and a very expensive procedure not only for the public schools, but for clinics and agencies as well. Often, school counselors find it necessary to refer needy parents and children to school clinics or private therapists. This practice also presents problems because clinics often have long waiting lists and frequent changes in personnel. In addition, schools and clinics seldom enjoy coordinated relationships. Therefore, many parents become disenchanted with the necessity of repeating the historical background of their problems and the stress of adjusting to a change in therapists.

The challenge of children who do not respond to treatment or the inadequate handling of psychological problems have necessitated that parent counseling, individually or in groups, be available in schools, clinics, and community agencies. The group counseling intervention has helped parents to become more understanding and more nurturant, and has improved communication and interaction between parent and child. The growing competence of the parent has resulted in improving the self-esteem of the child, and of the parents themselves. This gradually becomes evident through better academic grades and social performance of the child to the great satisfaction and relief of the parents. Thus the interpersonal atmosphere of the family is characterized by greater harmony and communication.

The preceding situation has motivated me to share with other interested professionals an accumulation of material successfully used with various kinds of parent groups over several years. Though this approach has been used in a school setting, it also has been used successfully in clinics and private agencies. Based upon parents' own evaluations, the group process experience has proven to be productive, efficient, and cost effective. In the event that parents need more help than the group process can offer, the trust and confidence gained through their exposure to the group usually motivates them to seek additional help. They will often request the leader's assistance in making a referral to other and more appropriate resources. In any case, a supportive alliance between parents and school usually results in better relations between home and school as well as between parent and child.

Formal prescreening of group participants is generally not possible in public schools, because participation is open to the parents of all children who are experiencing any kind of adjustment or learning problem. However, if the leader desires to screen participants, this can be done by using the registration sheet (see appendix), which lends itself to this purpose. Occasionally a very troubled parent will join a group. In such a case, it is the leader's responsibility to meet individually with the parent and discuss the parent's expectations from the group. According to the severity of the problem, the leader should point out the limitation of group counseling in an empathic and sensitive manner and kindly guide or refer the parent to a more appropriate resource that can help resolve the problem.

This guidebook describes an eclectic approach to parent group counseling. The contents have been research- and field-tested with different types of groups, but the participants have been primarily mothers or couples. The theoretical formulations are based on ego psychology, human relations training, and communication skills. The procedures presented are designed to strengthen the ego of both parents and children by improving insight, empathic understanding, and interpersonal skills as well as by providing specific parenting information, support, and respect. A combination of psychological and counseling theories (those of Sigmund Freud, Erik Erikson, Robert White, Jean Piaget, Jerome Kagan, Jerome Bruner, and John Bowlby, to name a few), human relations techniques, and educational approaches are used. The cognitive presentations often use bibliotherapy, and appropriate bibliographies are supplied. The human relations training and interpersonal communication skills development use role playing and are ongoing throughout the sessions.

An effort has been made to keep this guidebook simple, clear, easy to follow, and nonsexist. The material provided represents an accumulation of various theories from several experts in the fields of child development, group counseling, and human relations. I encourage counselors to keep abreast of new research and techniques and to feel free to supplement each module with current, significant material as it becomes available.

The fifteen meetings are outlined in a staccato style to provide the counselor with utmost freedom to give a personal cast to the group. The main topic is introduced by a brief paragraph that highlights the salient points to ensure maximum coverage as well as a smooth transition from one meeting to the next. It is assumed that the leader is well informed in theories of child development, family dynamics, and the group process. It is important to point out that the fluid nature of discussion and counseling groups often precludes strict adherence to the didactic presentation of the guidebook. Therefore, the counselor may not be able to cover all the topics as scheduled in the guidebook. Such flexibility is expected. The trained counselor can allow for this through adaptive techniques, and restrain the group from entering into irrelevant discussion areas. Specific suggestions are provided to maintain the group's focus on its stated goals throughout the five stages of the group process: structuring, exploration, transition, action, and termination. These stages (based on Gazda, 1971), are reflected in the organization of the meetings as follows:

Module 1:   Structuring (generally meetings one through three)

Module 2:   Exploration (generally meetings four through seven)

Module 3:   Transition (generally meetings eight through ten)

Module 4:   Action (generally meetings eleven through thirteen)

Module 5:   Termination (generally meetings fourteen and fifteen)

Introduction

It was Sigmund Freud who first theorized that the most severe and crippling adult personality disorders originated in childhood. "The capacity for enduring love, and the exercise of conscience, are not biological givens. They are achieved through the early partnership between the parent and child. The child who is deprived of this partnership in the early years, or experiences shifting, or unstable relationships during the formative period, suffers impairment of his capacity to love, to learn, to make decisions, to judge, and to abide by the laws of his society. *In effect he is deprived of his humanity*" (emphasis added).

In his 1969 book *Attachment and Loss,* John Bowlby writes, "What is believed to be essential for mental health is that the infant and young child should experience a warm, intimate and continuous relationship with his mother (or permanent mother substitute) in which BOTH find satisfaction and enjoyment." Later he states that "loss of mother figure either by itself, or in combination with other variables generates responses and processes that contribute to psychopathology, not only in childhood but sometimes remain active in older individuals. Among these disturbances are the tendency to make excessive demands on others, anxiety and anger when these demands are not met, dependency and hysteria and the inability to form deep or mutually satisfying interpersonal relationships."

Selma Fraiberg, in her 1977 book *Every Child's Birthright: In Defense of Mothering,* noted that studies done on children separated from their parents during World War II reveal that even these life-threatening situations were not as destructive to the cognitive and emotional development of the children who remained with their parents as they were to those who were separated from their parents.

Yet, incredible as it may seem, until recently, the process of parenting was thought of as natural and instinctive. Somehow, upon the birth of their first baby, the couple were magically and automatically invested with the capabilities of raising their child with nurturance, love, and sensitivity. The fact that many parents were inadequate, or often emotionally unprepared to accept the enormous responsibility of raising their child, was discounted and ignored. That these factors might affect their child's physical, emotional, social, and cognitive well-being was not even considered. Somehow, parenthood supposedly brought forth the proper maternal and paternal instincts, and one way or another the child would grow. Unfortunately, the instinct for parenting as such is often *not* enough. The increasing number of children who fail in school, or who suffer from emotional and social disturbances, and the increase in teenage crime, suicides, pregnancies, and runaways have all forced upon us the realization that parenting in today's society is at best a difficult process. At worst, it can be an experience rife with pain, feelings of failure, and a source of stress and disability for many families.

The modern U.S. family is subject to a wide range of conflicting pressures and uncertainties. Changing life-styles, and geographic and social mobility are characteristic of our times and tend to sever families from their traditional moorings, leaving them vulnerable and insecure. The increasing independence of women as they move away from the home to the world of outside work has relegated parenting to the status of a lesser occupation. Thus, parents far removed from other family members, cultural traditions of child-rearing have been challenged and have complicated the plight of the child in the process of forming human bonds and attachments. Psychological evidence arising from the study of human infancy affirms the primacy of these human bonds and attachments. This evidence has demonstrated unequivocally that for better or worse, parenting has an enormous and relatively permanent impact upon the developing personality and future destiny of the child.

Parenthood does not begin with the birth of a couple's first baby. It began when the parents themselves experienced the child-side of this relationship. Gradually they developed those concepts of parenting that they ultimately will put into use with their own children. Thus, parenthood begins with the level of awareness developed during their early childhood period and is moderated as they move on and away from the egocentric level. This awareness is also affected by other ongoing relationships that eventually are generalized by parents into the parent–child interaction in their own family.

In their relationship with their children, parents are assumed to possess superior knowledge, and to have the ability to maintain complete control and power over them. (No other human interaction is ascribed such capacities.) Realistically, this is not always the case, particularly with teenage parents or with those whose own parenting was inadequate. The model provided by their own parents is inextricably woven into their personalities and affects the mode of relating to one's own children. Thus, parents must be helped to increase their awareness to, and understanding of the importance of these early love bonds or attachments. They also need to understand the critical influence that the impact of their own personality has upon the developing child, and the probability that the child's development and personal destiny may be adversely affected.

Another significant point is the dynamic and changing nature of parenting. As children grow and develop in a supportive and trusting environment, they gradually establish competence and independence. This causes the balance of parental power and authority between parents and children to change continuously and to become renegotiable. Initially, parents are invested with full responsibility for their children until they come of age and can take charge of themselves. The dynamism of this unique relationship, with its responsibilities and changing demands, provides parents with opportunities for growth. This growth goes beyond the concepts of parenting developed during one's early childhood because growth is usually tempered by many experiences and other relationships.

Thus, the parent–child relationship is a mutual and reciprocal system. The quality of this relationship needs to be stable and clearly identified. The relationship transcends all the ups and downs of their mutual experiences, and involves their shared feelings and expectations. When conflicts cannot be resolved, differences in viewpoint should be shared and respected. How the parent and child act in dealing with these differences can be negotiated. Personal feelings are recognized and maintained, and actions are modified according to the best interests of both the child and the parent. Through this relationship parents become aware that they, too, are continually growing and learning. Parents grow in their capacity to reflect upon, understand, and accept the complexities of their personhood and those of the child. Thus, parenting becomes a process of personal growth that models and induces similar growth in the child.

Parent and child are two ultimately autonomous but interdependent members of the family system, a system that is vital and necessary for the child's security. This system runs on love, understanding, awareness, negotiation, compromise, and change, so that each member can continue to experience satisfaction and enhance mutual growth. Furthermore, the basis of all relationships between individuals is empathy. It is essential that the parent feel empathy for the child if the parent is to grow and develop, and before the child can, in turn, demonstrate empathy for the parent.

Because the child's first encounter with the world is through its parents, it is necessary for the parents to be aware of any perceived negative influences that their own parenting may have had that might endanger the healthy development of their child. When this happens parents should know that they may safely divest and overcome negative practices without shame or loss of self-esteem. Therefore, it is important that counselors, psychologists, and other professionals make their services known to parents and establish adequate and appropriate opportunities for parental growth and understanding. Group discussion and counseling has proven to be a creative process that helps parents to develop a secure bond with their children so that parenting can become a mutually satisfying, growth-producing experience for all.

It would be foolish to think that all emotional and psychological problems between parents and children will respond to this one approach. Some problems cannot and should not be handled in this way, as they may require intensive psychotherapy or other strategies. However, my experience, supported and validated by the many parents who have participated in group counseling, has established that this intervention results in improved awareness and sensitivity of most parents. This in turn makes a positive difference in the quality of their family life. Parental growth, understanding, and cooperation not only affect the emotional, social, and cognitive growth of their children, but improve their own self-esteem and help to formulate better home and school relationships. Naturally there will be those families who will require individual and long-term attention.

The meetings outlined in this guidebook are intended to guide leaders in helping parents view child development as an outcome of interaction between parents and the environment and to increase their awareness of feelings and attitudes. Discussions focus on the children as dynamic entities who are in continual process with parents, with others, and with themselves. The child's conscious and unconscious feelings in relating to others are emphasized through actions, perceptions, and physical characteristics. These can be identified and described at any point in the developmental continuum. As a result of these experiences and with the nurturant and empathic support of parents, children ultimately achieve a deeper understanding of themselves and others. Thus, the child's emotional, social, and intellectual potential can be maximized, and the child can become a more productive and integrated member of society.

In addition, the methodology and procedures described encourage parental growth and are intended to improve parental communication skills and interpersonal relations between them and their children. These can assist in the development of family closeness and unity as well as mutual self-esteem.

The Basics
of Parent Counseling

Goals of Parent Counseling Discussion Groups

Parent counseling groups attempt to prevent and alleviate suffering for both the parents and their children. This type of intervention enlightens parents on issues of normal child development, and increases their awareness of the meaning of child behavior and the role that feelings play on their coping strategies. It improves their interpersonal communication and problem-solving skills, and enhances their self-esteem. It enables parents to reduce conflict in the home, provide a nurturing and loving environment that encourages their children's full growth and unfoldment at a time when they are most vulnerable, dependent, and impressionable.

Generally, parents participating in a discussion group want to achieve and formulate their own goals. However, there are some general goals that the leader/counselor should keep in mind. These professionals should

- Help parents develop an awareness of the impact of their feelings upon parenting and how these affect their children's development and behavior.

- Help parents to realistically assess their parenting style in terms of its adequacy and its effectiveness in achieving *their* goals with their children.

- Help parents to understand the basic developmental stages all children go through and the associated tasks to be achieved at each stage.

- Deepen parental understanding of how children's mastery of each sequential task will ultimately assist them to achieve wholesome growth, personality integration, self-esteem, and personal competence.

- Assist parents to modify and expand their parenting style in order that their goals for their children are not in conflict with the basic nature of their children.

- Facilitate discussion of parent–child issues, concerns, and conflicts to improve parental understanding of their own needs and goals and of the child striving towards maturity.

- Provide parents with interpersonal communication experiences to help them develop mutual problem-solving skills and the techniques that eliminate destructive and unhealthy family interaction.

- Encourage parents to explore, recognize, and discuss their feelings, attitudes, and concerns; to develop and expand their awareness, insight, perspective, and improve their own expertise as human beings.
- Assist parents to take constructive and positive action toward their own growth as well as on pertinent family issues and problems.
- Validate participants as parents and human beings who are trying to do their best, and to increase their own self-confidence and self-esteem.

Group Recruitment and Organization

The recruitment of parents and organization of groups depends on several factors, such as

1. target population;
2. group size;
3. timing;
4. available place;
5. fees;
6. number and length of meetings;
7. motivational strategies.

Recruitment

The counselor's efforts are directed at the following groups.

- Parents whose child has had a core team evaluation as provided by Public Law 94-142, which includes a physical, psychological, and educational assessment, and whose child's individual educational plan recommends counseling.
- Parents referred by teachers or principals because their children present learning or adjustment problems that are not responding to ordinary school resources.
- Parents whose preschool children's kindergarten screening reveals them to be "at risk," and who desire help.
- Parents who are concerned about their children's academic achievement and/or social problems and are seeking some kind of guidance.
- Parents whose children are retarded or disabled and are seeking support and further understanding of their children's problems and wish to develop behavior management skills.
- Single or divorced parents who feel overwhelmed by their dual role and are seeking guidance to improve their parenting skills.

1. *Target Population.* The composition of a group does not necessarily have to be homogeneous. However, groups who have something in common usually work well together. It is advisable, for example, to have single parents with nuclear parents, but not

advisable to have preschool parents with parents of high-school-age children because their concerns are often too far apart to promote a common discussion. Parents with sharp educational and socioeconomic differences also may not mix well. However, divorced or widowed parents are often compatible with intact families and they seem to profit from their acceptance and help. Primarily, participants should have problems in common, and should seek some way of coping with them.

2. *Group Size*

- There should be no less than four and no more than twenty people in any one group.
- The optimum number in terms of cost-effectiveness and stimulation is between ten and fourteen.
- Inevitably a few participants will drop out, so the leader can accept a few more people than are needed for each group.

Group size should be determined by the number of *parental units*. A parental unit can be one or both parents. Twenty parental units consisting entirely of single-family representatives (which could include divorced, single, separated, or widowed persons) are different from ten couples (twenty persons when both mother and father are in attendance). In any case ten couples are much easier to work with than twenty single parents. Also, four single parents are a group—but four persons comprising two parental units are really too small to be a group.

3. *Timing*

- Evening meetings are usually scheduled when both parents wish to attend together or when participants have to work during the day.
- Morning or midday meetings are often desirable for parents of preschool or elementary children, or for those parents at home during the day.
- The day of the week selected depends upon such factors as the schedule of community activities including civic, religious, or social commitments that may involve parents on a regular basis.
- Initially the counselor tries to offer a choice of days and times, even though these may be scheduled to meet in different places; Friday is typically not a good day to select.
- However, it is often better for the counselor to select the day, time, and place for each group. In this case at least two options should be offered. The counselor presumably will be leading more than one group.

4. *Available Place.* The meeting place depends upon the availability of space in the clinic, local school system, or similar facility.

- The leader needs to consider the number of participants and the possibilities of seating the group around a table. Classroom seating style or seating in an auditorium is to be avoided at all costs because it is not conducive to eye contact, intimacy, and friendliness.

- The counselor's office may be suitable if space permits.
- The school or public library may be used when not otherwise scheduled. The public library usually will lend its function or conference room as a community service.
- School counselors will find that principals and administrators are usually helpful in offering conference or teachers' rooms; these will often have facilities for making coffee or using tape recorders (if the group decides this is permissible).
- Heating, lighting, ventilation, and accessibility to exits should be considered for the group's comfort and safety.
- Avoid rooms with loudspeakers, telephones, or people passing through, as these interfere with confidentiality and freedom of expression.
- Before meetings alert the custodian so that parents will not be locked out of or in the building. Also, corridors and hallways should be lighted to insure safety of the participants.

5. Fees

- The fee charged will depend upon going rates and the clients' ability to pay. Often Blue Shield and other insurance contracts will cover subscribers. However, public meeting facilities will charge a rental fee and the counselor will need to assess each participant accordingly.

6. Number and Length of Meetings

- The materials in this guidebook are designed to extend over a period of fifteen weekly meetings. Attempts to condense the period to ten to twelve meetings have led to problems with termination; most participants have requested additional meetings.
- The action or role-playing stage is particularly useful but most groups are not prepared for this until the information or transition stage has been thoroughly absorbed.
- Even after fifteen meetings, many groups like the support of meeting on a monthly basis to exchange feelings and views and to "brush up" their new found skills.

This latter practice is up to the leader's depth of commitment or available time.

- Meetings run for two hours, with a brief five-minute break.

7. Motivational Strategies. In a school setting, consult with the administrators and teachers about the feasibility of counseling services for the parents of children with problems. In an agency, consult with parents and suggest their participation in a group. Discuss feasibility of client referrals by other colleagues.
   The leader should send invitational letters (for format see appendix A).

- The leader helps the principal or director to draft and send a warm, cordial, honest letter describing the service and inviting the parents' participation in a group especially for them.

- The letter may be signed by the school principal and the clinic director or counselor (or both of the latter).
- The letter should include the specific date and time of meetings, a simplified return response, and the group leader's name.
- The letter should stress the importance of both fathers' and mothers' participation.
- The letter should offer the parent the opportunity to attend an alternative or future group in the event that the timing is not convenient.
- Unanswered letters should be followed up by a phone call by the counselor, or designee, to determine the level of interest and whether the parent wishes an opportunity to join a future group, or whether individualized services are required.

Phone contacts are an important follow-up tool.

- The counselor may use a simple phone call in situations when principals or evaluation team chairpersons offer a list of parents who have already indicated their interest in participating in a group.
- The same options and explanations should be given to the parent and a letter indicating date, time, and place of the meetings should be sent to confirm the parent's participation in the designated group.

Word-of-mouth referrals also play an important role.

- Many parents who have heard about the groups from other participants will call to ask about this service.
- The counselor accepts these people into the appropriate group and sends a letter indicating time and place of the meetings to confirm the parents' participation in the designated group.

Parents may be preinterviewed, but this is a difficult practice to implement in a public school, primarily because it is assumed that the population consists of "normal" people whose problems are hurting them or their children. Clinics and agencies may be more selective. But in general, the services of a public school have to be equally available to all parents.

Organization

Organizing a parent counseling group requires some motivational strategies and, in a school setting, the cooperation of other professionals. The counselor must be extremely sensitive to the disposition of administrators and the parents he or she wishes to motivate. Although most administrators, teachers, and the general public now appreciate the need for parent counseling, assisting the leader to reach the parents does require their time, attention, and support. In addition, it is important that parents not be made to feel like failures because their children have undergone a core team evaluation or have some kind of problem in or out of school. On the *contrary, group counseling should be offered to parents as another service by the school, clinic, or agency that can assist them to help their children to function better.* It must enhance the recipients' skills just as do speech therapy, remedial reading, and the like.

General Procedures

An outline of the structure and procedure for each of the fifteen meetings is presented in this guidebook. Obviously, the first meeting should be exceptionally well planned since it is crucial to the success of subsequent meetings. Even though parents' participation in a group is voluntary, initially there is a tendency on their part to be somewhat apprehensive and insecure. Their unfamiliarity or inexperience with the group process causes some reluctance and embarrassment and it is difficult for them to imagine that they can discuss personal concerns with total strangers.

Therefore, the counselor must be sensitive to this factor and help the participants relax by being empathic, reassuring, and relaxed in order to set a positive tone. The greeting should be genuine and friendly. The self-introduction should include background, training, and experience as well as some personal information, within the limits of professionalism. The counselor should be a warm, understanding, and empathic leader who places broad professional training and experience at their disposal to facilitate discussions that lead to insight and understanding of their concerns. The counselor enables them to mobilize their combined wisdom and newly gained insights toward the resolution of the problems that motivated their participation in the group.

The counselor is not an all-knowing or final authority. Rather, he or she shares the knowledge and information inherent to the discipline; offers emotional support and empathic understanding; elicits the expression of feelings and attitudes, both positive and negative; clarifies and synthesizes thoughts and feelings; guides group members to reflect upon and assess these feelings in terms of the topics presented to them; and encourages the realignment of these feelings so that they may remove, overcome, or come to terms with the emotional blocks that have precluded the achievement of individual goals. But the leader is also able to support responses by citing research and sound psychological theories.

In general all meetings follow a similar procedure except that the didactic presentation changes with the introduction of the sequential developmental stages of children's development and related topics. All subsequent meetings begin with the leader's greeting the members and allowing questions to emanate from the group. Usually these questions are based on the presentation made, on the printed handouts distributed the previous week, as well as on accounts of particular circumstances or encounters occurring between parent and child that relate to the topic.

Insofar as possible, the leader avoids giving "solutions" to the problems presented. Rather, parents are helped to understand the dynamics involved in the situation. With the participation of other group members, the leader assists them to formulate an acceptable strategy for handling the problem. For this reason role-playing is introduced as early as possible in the meetings. This facilitates the introduction of human relations and communication skills in problem solving. It permits the counselor to emphasize the role that feelings play in all interpersonal relations, whether they be between adults or between parents and children.

Presenting the Developmental Stages

The developmental stages outlined in this guidebook are primarily based on the work of Erik Erikson, John Bowlby, Robert White, and Jean Piaget. I believe that all parent groups need some knowledge of the important developmental stages of childhood in order to understand the meaning of behavior and what is appropriate at different stages. It is a well-accepted psychological fact that the unresolved issues of childhood continue to surface in different forms as the child grows, and that these can present serious problems at adolescence and later in life. Therefore, it is recommended that the counselor not overlook the initial presentations when working with parents of preadolescents and/or teenagers. However, the counselor should carefully explain this to the parents, and should be able to relate the problems they bring up for discussion to the unmet needs of the appropriate stage.

For parent groups of preschool or elementary-school-age children it is recommended that the counselor emphasize the following five stages.

1. Trust vs. mistrust
2. Competence vs. inadequacy
3. Autonomy vs. shame and doubt
4. Initiative vs. guilt
5. Industry vs. inferiority

These stages usually involve the basic issues from infancy through latency. The presentations of these stages are interlaced with related issues such as attachment, dependence, independence, loss, play, peer group relations, socialization, emergence of self, fears, discipline, sexuality, and self-esteem.

When conducting groups for parents of adolescents, the counselor should include two additional stages that cover the crucial issues for this age group:

6. Identity vs. role diffusion
7. Intimacy vs. isolation

The related early childhood issues mentioned above continue to be used and expanded upon, specifically, development of self-concept, independence, separation, identity, sexuality, and occupational choice. In addition, the counselor emphasizes peer group and social pressures, identity, intimacy, vocational and educational choices, mating, family dynamics, stress, and depression. Basic information on each of these developmental stages is presented in the outline of the meetings. Also, the important points and concepts are highlighted at the meetings, and also through the handouts (to ensure full coverage).

Specific training in identification of feelings and responding to feelings helps parents to develop problem-solving techniques that initially they can test out safely within the group. Experimentation with different strategies is both exciting and frustrating and the leader helps parents to come to their own understanding in deciding what they can or cannot live with. The interaction within the group becomes truly *supportive* and *therapeutic* and the counselor encourages this gently and consistently.

Preparing for Termination

Before the fourteenth meeting, the leader begins to help the group accept the fact of the oncoming termination of their weekly meetings. Most groups show dismay and some anxiety about this prospect. They are elated by their success but also fearful of their ability to maintain their newfound insight and strategies. They fear reverting to old ingrained ways and losing their newfound skills. The leader needs to express confidence in their ability to maintain self-awareness and to retain the gains made. Discussion is encouraged and role-playing is offered to see what might happen once participants are "on their own." The leader will also help to establish a liaison between the group and community resources such as the library, church and community groups, parent advisory councils, and the like. The leader should encourage maintaining contact with each other—much as self-help groups do. Whenever feasible, monthly follow-up meetings should be arranged. Finally, the leader will refer them again to the bibliography and encourage bibliotherapy (use of appropriate literature in a therapeutic way). Arrangements for this can be made by eliciting the cooperation of the local library.

Evaluation

Built-in evaluation is provided for, first by the registration sheet (see appendix A), and secondly by use of the sentence completion survey given at the second and last meetings (see appendix A). The evaluation on the registration sheet (which is also completed at the final meeting) enables participants to look at the overall effect that the meetings have had upon their goals. It also enables them to evaluate the quality of the leadership and interaction, and invites their comments (both positive and negative). Thus, the parents feel they have some input on how future parent programs can be of most service. The leader, in turn, can use these results to improve future programs. If desired, the upper section of this same registration sheet can be used as a screening device.

The sentence completion survey (given before and after the series of meetings) enables the parents themselves to observe whether there has been any shift or change in their attitudes, feelings, and perceptions of the parent–child interaction. This is especially useful because parents are evaluating themselves—they are not being evaluated by the leader. However, use of the sentence completion survey is optional and participants may elect to keep these results or return them to the leader.

Parent Handouts

The handouts offer cognitive information to help parents understand the topics outlined at each meeting. Their use is highly recommended and they generally stimulate parental questions, concerns, and discussion. Parents also use these as bibliotherapy long after the sessions are over. The suggested titles should be given to the parents at the end of each meeting in preparation for the next. However, the leader may decide which related topics to distribute at any one meeting. This is usually determined by the questions and concerns brought up by the parents. These materials can be supplemented by other updated literature as well as additional pertinent research.

Meeting 1
Introductory Procedures

A. General points.
    1. Plan the agenda carefully and thoughtfully—all needed materials should be ready.
    2. The meeting place should be ready—seating, coatracks, etc.
    3. Start on time.
    4. Arrange seating around a table whenever possible.
    5. Offer refreshments—coffee, juice, etc.
    6. Participants should not exceed twenty people (ten to fourteen is ideal).
    7. Length of daytime meetings should be 1½ to 2 hours; evening meetings, 1 to 2½ hours.
B. Beginning the meeting.
    1. Welcome, opening remarks, and self-introduction.
    2. Circulate attendance sheet for members to sign (see appendix A). This will be the basis for the telephone tree to be given to all members in the group.
    3. Outline rationale and purpose for group.
C. Exercises.
    1. Listening Exercise. This will illustrate one of the skills to be improved upon by the group.
        a. Every other participant forms a diad with the person seated to the right.
        b. Each participant shares with the partner as much personal information about self and family as can be told within a *two*-minute interval.
        c. Invite each member of the diads to introduce the partner by telling the group all he can remember.
        d. Partners will score the accuracy of each other's rendition.
        e. Leader will comment upon the difficulties inherent to listening and hearing each other—particularly under stress.
        f. Leader allows for brief group discussion.
    2. Registration.
        a. Distribute and explain registration sheets.
        b. Encourage honesty in stating the present goals that the participants wish to achieve.
        c. Explain evaluation criteria at the bottom of the sheet. Sheets will be returned and completed by the participants at the final meeting to give them the opportunity to evaluate the leader and their own group experience.

3. Establish structure and rules for subsequent meetings.
   a. Leader stresses the issues of confidentiality, honesty, mutual respect, speaking in turn, and regularity of attendance.
   b. Group establishes rules for attendance, provisions for holiday make-ups, length of meetings, provisions for refreshments, breaks during meeting, smoking, "telephone tree" in case of cancellation or emergency, transportation needs (share-a-ride), and so forth.
4. Exercise to establish mutuality of concerns.
   a. Leader requests participants to break up and form into groups of three to five people (depending upon the size of total group).
   b. Each group selects a recorder.
   c. Leader asks groups to discuss "What bugs/upsets me most about my children?" for a five-minute interval.
   d. Each recorder then reports on the group's discussion.
   e. Leader comments on similarity of concerns in each group and allows a brief discussion.
5. Exercise in identification of present coping strategies.
   a. Leader requests each group to reconvene for another five minutes using the same recorder.
   b. Discuss strategies currently used by parents to cope with behaviors previously identified and results being achieved.
   c. Leader calls upon recorders to report strategies used and results.
   d. Leader allows brief comments and inquiry by group.
6. Exercise in increasing awareness to the origin of reported coping strategies.
   a. Leader reconvenes same groups with same recorders for a three-minute interval.
   b. Leader asks groups to discuss "Which of the identified coping strategies was used by your own parents during your youth?"
   c. Leader encourages participants to identify their feelings as youths when these methods were used on them and whether their parents got similar results.
   d. Recorder will report findings and feelings.
   e. Leader will encourage discussion of feelings.
D. Introduction of information topics.
1. Leader distributes topical agenda and handouts for next meetings.
2. Leader comments on handouts—initiates discussion, invites comments, and answers questions.
3. Leader should emphasize the following:
   a. Praise and validate the parent as a dynamic force who has an extremely critical influence upon the developing child.
   b. Necessity to understand infancy in order to make sense of future developmental stages and problems.
   c. Infancy is universal and the bedrock of personality formation.
   d. Long-range effects of early childhood experience upon self-esteem and personal destiny.
   e. Importance of parental understanding of childhood developmental stages upon their parenting style.

      f.   The importance of feelings in learning.

      g.   Understanding behavior as a demonstration of feelings.

      h.   Importance of listening, understanding, and responding to feelings.

      i.   Effect of communication patterns—giving examples of destructive and empathic responses.

      j.   Awareness of parental stages and their effect on child.

      k.   Awareness of social and economic pressures on parenting.

E.   Preparation for next meeting.

   1.   Leader urges parents to read and keep all handouts in a notebook for future reference. Distributes parents' agenda.

   2.   Leader invites parents to bring in and share their own experiences for discussional purposes.

   3.   Leader suggests that parents can also contribute to any material they find on children's growth and development for the meetings.

F.   Suggested parent handouts for meeting 2.

   1.   Dynamics of Parenthood

   2.   Trust vs. Mistrust

   3.   Physical Tasks of the Newborn

   4.   Tasks of the Older Infant

   5.   The Emergence of Self in Infancy

   6.   Transitions in Early Childhood

Note: The techniques listed under item C initiate the human relations training and problem-solving skills that will be part of every meeting. The exercises described have proven to be very effective in "breaking the ice" and decreasing communication barriers between participants. They help to establish an atmosphere of friendliness and togetherness that permits members to get to know and to begin to trust each other and the leader. Feelings of inadequacy or failure are dissipated or minimized as participants realize the commonality of their problems. A sense of "not being alone," of sharing, and of listening to each other helps to form a real working group. As these feelings are internalized they become supportive and therapeutic.

TOPICAL AGENDA AND
HANDOUT SUBJECTS

Developmental Stages (from Infancy through Adolescence)

Trust vs. Mistrust

Dynamics of Parenthood
Trust vs. Mistrust
Physical Tasks of the Newborn
Tasks of the Older Infant
The Emergence of Self in Infancy
Transitions in Early Childhood

Competence vs. Inadequacy

Competence vs. Inadequacy
Tasks of the Toddler: Psychological and Behavioral Characteristics
Peer Group Socialization and Play
The Toddler and the Preschool Age
What Children Should Know before Entering School
Childhood Sexuality
The Development of Attitudes

Autonomy vs. Shame and Doubt

Autonomy vs. Shame and Doubt
Antecedents of Self-Concept
Differences between Children and Adults
The Basic Needs of All Children
Fears
What to Tell Your Children about Santa Claus
Discipline
Helping Children to Deal with Death and Loss

Initiative vs. Guilt

Initiative vs. Guilt
TV's Influence on Children
Rules for Keeping Poisons and Children Apart
Responding to Children's Sexuality
Some Reasons for Poor Eating Habits
Characteristics of Young School-Age Children
The Father's Role
When a Child Begins School
Be Their Mother, Not Their Servant

Industry vs. Inferiority

Industry vs. Inferiority
Raising Children
Getting Along with Your Child's Teachers
The Angry Child
Feelings of Guilt
Stress

Identity vs. Role Diffusion—(For Parents of Adolescents)

Identity vs. Role Diffusion
Helping Children to Learn
What's Good for Your Marriage Is Good for Your Children!
Guidelines for Parenting

Intimacy vs. Isolation—For Parents of Adolescents

Intimacy vs. Isolation
Are Your Expectations of Your Children Realistic?
Good Study Tips
Helping Children Make Career Plans
Sexuality and Your Teenager
At Home with Your Teenager

Meeting 2
Trust vs. Mistrust

A. Greetings and opening remarks.
    1. Participants check off attendance sheet.
    2. Leader briefly summarizes previous meeting.
    3. Leader refers to parent handouts and briefly expands on them as related to infants' needs and parental roles.
    4. Short discussion to lead into new topic.
B. Exercise—sentence completion survey (see appendix).
    1. Leader distributes and explains sentence completion survey.
    2. Leader emphasizes that this activity is useful but optional.
    3. Leader also explains that the sentence stems should be completed honestly, briefly, and spontaneously.
    4. Current answers reflect the feelings and attitudes the participants have now about the topics therein.
    5. Self-identification on the survey is optional. However, participants should use some identifying symbol so that they can recognize their own surveys at the end of the fifteen weekly sessions.
    6. At termination they will be asked to complete another identical survey.
        a. The present survey will be returned to them.
        b. They will then have the opportunity to compare their current answers with the answers they will give at the end of fifteen weeks.
    7. The comparison between these two sets of answers will reveal whether their attitudes and feelings have changed in any way.
    8. Return of the surveys to the leader is optional.
C. Topical presentation: The importance of infancy and the development of trust vs. mistrust.
    1. The presentation should be delivered in open-ended fashion; parents should feel free to interrupt with questions and comments.
D. Discussion highlights.
    1. Birth trauma is assuaged by reception from the mother, her loving care, and unqualified acceptance.
    2. The infant is initially unaware of his separateness of even his body.

3. The infant is totally dependent on his parents for satisfaction of his needs and survival.
4. The infant's understanding of the world is shaped by internalization of his feelings about realities, mutual expectations, and anticipations.
5. Communication is through behavioral cues that the infant trusts the parents to understand.
6. The infant internalizes and responds to cues emanating from mother that sometimes cause him tension.
7. The infant is an active and reactive being, and is initially egocentric; he responds to his inner feelings, and then gradually to the environment.
8. An infant's attachment behavior (bonding) anchors his future feelings of security. His future sense of individuation, competence and independence is based upon feelings of security.
9. Parenting revolves around the polarities of attachment–separation–independence.
10. The father has a subtle but important role. His love for the mother enables her to provide their baby with genuine and unqualified affection.
11. The father's role continues to expand as he maintains the moral tone of the family and later assists in the development of child's sexual identity.

E. Human relations training.
1. The leader cites and describes pertinent studies supporting above points (for example, Gerald Stechler, J. Bowlby, R. Spitz, and H. Harlow).
2. The leader initiates discussion using parents' personal experience.
3. Sample lead-ins.
    a. "Would anyone like to react to any of the points mentioned so far?"
    b. "Would you like to tell us more about that?"
    c. "Would you tell us how that made you feel?"
    d. "How does it seem to you?"
    e. "What worries you most about _____ ?"
    f. "Can you give us an example?"
4. The leader practices human relations training and listening skills by accurately responding to feelings expressed.
5. The leader maintains eye contact and listens carefully and empathically.

F. Preparation for next meeting.
1. The leader distributes handouts to parents.
2. The leader makes appropriate comments and distributes the sentence completion survey.
3. Discussion on the newborn and older infant often goes into more than one meeting.

G. Suggested parent handouts for meeting 3.
1. Competence vs. Inadequacy
2. Tasks of the Toddler: Psychological and Behavioral Characteristics
3. Peer Group Socialization and Play
4. The Toddler and Preschool Age
5. What Children Should Know before Entering School
6. Childhood Sexuality
7. The Development of Attitudes

Background for topical presentation: The emphasis is on the role that feelings play in all aspects of development, especially in infancy because the child is not born knowing. Every normal child is endowed with a body, five senses, and the potential for intelligence. Initially, the newborn is not aware of his separateness from his mother. When he is catapulted into the world his potential to think, see, touch, hear, and taste is yet undeveloped because he lacks experience. It is through feelings that he can express and know the meaning of hunger, pain, comfort, and the like. As he experiences the love and nurturance of the mothering person and as his needs are met, the other senses assist him in achieving a sense of inner homeostasis. This enables him to increasingly trust the environment and the people in it especially his parents. Now he can begin to perceive, differentiate, incorporate, and integrate what he sees, feels, thinks, and touches. The child begins to apply meaning to these functions. When this process meets the infant's needs fairly consistently and with minimal frustration, he feels validated and worthwhile. To the extent that the infant is loved, cuddled, and talked to, he will feel free to reach out, explore, perceive, and take in and respond to the world around him. The child who lacks consistent nurturance, warmth, and affection finds it difficult to trust his environment as well as his own instincts and feelings.

DYNAMICS OF PARENTHOOD

Parents transmit their values from one generation to another through the family system and thus guide their children to develop the capacity to cope with their environment.

Parents are the child's first teachers and introduce life's practical needs through family patterns and values. They teach the young countless everyday life skills such as how to eat with a fork and knife; to observe numerous rules of hygiene and personal safety; and to use various objects such as the telephone, radio, and television. In the course of the family's daily routine children learn right from wrong, good from bad, when to laugh or not to laugh, how to care for body, soul, and psyche.

Long before exposure to such academic fields as literature, mathematics, or science, it is essential that children learn basic life skills and social responsibility. These include self-restraint; how to dress; how to use money; how to listen; how to relax; how to be friendly, personable, guarded, or open; how to love and accept love; how to respect the family and community; how to adjust to changes or new ideas and to give and to take; how to forgive, reward, and judge; how to admit to fear; and how to think for themselves.

Children not only bear a strong physical resemblance to their parents, but generally imitate parental ways of walking or talking, gesturing, thinking, and even complaining. Although they will learn things from many other people, *parents are their first and most important teachers*. They pass along the family's traditions and values through their speech, manners, beliefs, awareness, and other subtle aspects of their daily interaction. The role of parent–educator has historically been of vital importance. Therefore, it is important that parents realize and *use their power constructively and effectively*. Of course no one can be perfect, nor is perfection required. However, if you can teach your child to pray, to trust you and herself, and to relate to others, you are competent! If you can explain to her/him about fire and rain, and the moon and the sky, you are a fine teacher! If you can help her to deal with her fears, and explain your own actions toward her, you are great! If you permit your child to be curious, to ask questions, to try things out, and even to fail, while giving her all your support in the process of her becoming able and competent, then you are wonderful! And, if above all this, you can show her your love so that she can feel it, then you do not need a college degree! You are providing all the needs for growth, for survival, and for self-respect.

Self-reliant, cooperative, and productive children grow in stable and trusting homes in which both parents are actively and consistently supportive and encouraging. Children grow wherever limits are defined and discipline is by guidance and example, and not just by precept, or punishment; they grow where they are valued, encouraged, and allowed to go forth to make their own lives, but are always welcome to return.

Conversely, disturbed, difficult, and unhappy children often come from disturbed and difficult homes, where discipline has been insensitive, inconsistent or inappropriate, or where (sometimes unwittingly) neglect, rejection, excessive punishment, or even abandonment have taken place. Very often, inept parenting comes from those parents whose own childhood was difficult and thereby has handicapped their ability to be adequate parents to their own children. Parents who have suffered serious deprivation in their childhood often find it difficult to understand and cope with the behavior of their own children.

Consultation with professionals is advised when parents feel the need to gain insight and training because of their inability to understand and to deal with their children's problems. The goal would be to develop objectivity, sensitivity, and appropriate parenting skills.

Parents have a very important role in the education and development of children. They have the right to be the authority for their children, provided this authority is not abused or destructive to the child's emerging individuality. They are the teachers and models for most of what is important to the young. In a million ways parents assist their children to know and to develop. Learning begins at birth and is an interactive process that continues in a constant and subtle manner all through life. Because parental influence is so subtle, institutional teaching has ignored it in maximizing the child's ability to learn. Its value has only recently been acknowledged by researchers and educators. Today more than ever home and family are recognized as having more influence on a child's social and academic achievement and personal destiny than any other social institution!

As parents you have the power to prepare your children to meet life's problems and challenges and to make the world better for themselves and ultimately for humanity.

TRUST VS. MISTRUST

Erik Erikson identifies the first stage of emotional development as a sense of trust. It tends to correspond to the oral stage in classical psychoanalytic theory. It begins at birth and develops progressively throughout the first year of life. Presumably, during this period the infant emerges into a new dimension of social interaction that involves basic *trust* at the one extreme and *mistrust* at the other. The degree to which the child will be able to trust the world, other people, and himself depends to a large extent upon the quality of the care that he receives from the mother. The infant whose needs are met as they arise, whose discomforts are quickly attended to, and who is cuddled, fondled, played with, and talked to is likely to feel that the world is a safe place and that people are helpful and dependable, and that he is loved and wanted. However, when the infant's care is inconsistent, inadequate, and rejecting, a sense of basic mistrust is fostered that generates attitudes of fear, suspicion, and anxiety toward the world in general and people in particular. Unless intercepted, these feelings will continue through his life and affect later stages of development.

It is important to point out that the issue of basic trust versus mistrust (as is true for all the later dimensions) is not resolved once and for all during the first year of life. It continues to occur again at each successive stage of development. There is both *hope* and *danger* in this. The child who may have developed a sense of mistrust and fears the environment may eventually come to trust a particular teacher or person who is kind, loving, and accepting, and who takes the trouble to be self trustworthy. If these new experiences are consistent, they will help the child to mitigate his early mistrust. On the other hand, the child who comes through infancy with a vital sense of trust may have his sense of mistrust activated at a later stage. For example, when parents become divorced or separated, the child may feel guilty and/or betrayed by the very people he needs and loves. His sense of trust is weakened and he resorts to mistrusting all adults.

This point may be illustrated by the experience of a four-year-old boy being seen at a clinic because his adoptive parents of six months wanted to return him to the agency. They claimed he was unresponsive, unloving, and unlovable, took things, and could not be trusted. He was indeed a cold and apathetic child who appeared indifferent and uncaring. About a year after his illegitimate birth he had been given up by his mother. He had been shunted back and forth among several foster homes. Initially he kept trying hard to relate to the people in the various foster homes. However, these relationships never had a chance to develop because he was always moved at just the time when he was beginning to feel secure. These events were very shattering to his weak ego and caused deep insecurity. He finally gave up trying to reach out to others, because the inevitable separations hurt too much and he felt he could not trust anyone—not even himself.

Based on "Erik Erikson's Eight Stages of Man," by David Elkind, New York Times Magazine, *5 April 1970.*

Physical Tasks of the Newborn

A. Newborns gradually accept and adjust to life outside the womb.
B. They develop appropriate physical responses (learn to suck or take in).
    1. They learn to cope with the mechanics of life: eating, sleeping, crying, and other bodily functions.
    2. Body needs are urgent—biologic unity with the mother is intense, and the newborn is not aware of her/his separateness from his/her mother.
    3. Reflexes dominate—movements are random and unfocused, and are not oriented to time or space.
    4. Newborns respond to mouth, oral and tactile stimuli, primarily physical reactions.
    5. The newborn is physiologically unstable—body needs dominate as the immature digestive system and other needs can cause distress; the newborn grows and changes rapidly.
C. Newborns develop appropriate physical responses.
    1. They are completely dependent or helpless.
    2. They exhibit low frustration tolerance or lack of patience.
    3. Newborns are noncognitive—they express needs instinctually; feelings predominate; they cannot think; they lack experience.
    4. Sensory modalities are important: feeling, touching, listening, tasting, and seeing—colors begin to register.
    5. Emergence of idiosyncratic patterns; modes of responding, relating, and reacting are emerging.
    6. Begins to imitate sounds, actions, and tries them out.

TASKS OF THE OLDER INFANT

A. Develops more self-control and self-reliance.
   1. Physiologically more stable, adapts to night and day, and to routines of eating, waking, and sleeping.
   2. Heightened voluntary motor activity and exploration of body parts—movements less random; exhibits more control over extremities and head.
B. Attachment behavior very evident; begins to prefer mother to others; values others and mother.
   1. Higher tolerance level and more patient, can wait to have needs met, recognizes mothering person's voice.
   2. Better control of instinctual needs—experience tells him he will be fed or picked up; learns to trust others.
   3. Strong selective tie to mother—knows others but prefers mother.
   4. Differentiates strangers—will cry when picked up by them.
   5. Outburst of negativism and anger when crossed; differentiates own wishes from those of others.
C. Emergence of developmental, psychological, social, and cognitive progress.
   1. Verbality increases; play and sensory–motor behavior evident; engages and responds to play; babbles; listens to own voice and voices of others.
   2. Social responses discernible; joyful in play; smiles; sounds acquire meanings.
D. Assimilates experience daily and develops increased capacity to wait, to postpone gratification, and to accept substitutes.
   1. Establishes symbiotic relationship with mother—cannot differentiate himself from mother or his own body parts.
   2. Cries when distressed: this is the first form of reaching out to environment; emotional bonding continues.
   3. Functions egocentrically—unaware of what others think and feel, responds only to needs within.
   4. Develops trust in ministering adult (usually mother).
   5. Begins to expect things, a first sign of trust and feelings of security.

THE EMERGENCE OF SELF IN INFANCY

The infant feels she is *all* because she is so new and so innocent and so "not knowing." This phenomenon is often referred to as the "omnipotency of infancy." The infant exists in the present because she does not *know* the past and she cannot conceptualize the future. Her sense of time is not developed.

Gradually she becomes aware of the world as her dwelling place, unless she is made to feel rejected and cut off by indifference from her caretakers. Her being brings order into the world. When she is nurtured, valued, and lovingly responded to by her parents, she develops responsiveness. When she feels safe she reaches out by touching, grasping, and feeling, and makes connections with life. Through her feelings and developing cognitive awareness, the infant builds bridges to objects and bonds herself to her mother and then to other people.

Slowly she differentiates between what is *under* her skin and what is *outside* her body; she begins to develop a sense of self, and then a sense of others. She learns to separate herself from objects and people, but she also learns to stay whole, to remain connected, or to stay related, as long as she is cherished and valued for being herself.

Thus, as the child grows in a healthy and nurturant environment, she reaches out to grasp the world and time. She develops an increasing capacity to convey and to receive meaning from experience. She expects responses from the people around her and in turn responds to them. Thus, a two-way social interaction develops between the child and her environment. Even as she separates herself from that to which she responds, she simultaneously remains related because she gradually internalizes its effects, and begins to derive meaning from it.

In the very act of becoming aware of herself as a separate individual entity, she develops her capacity for relatedness. This capacity will serve her throughout her life. Isolation and alienation are terrifying experiences because they deprive the child of her own self-awareness. In relatedness there is peace and the hope of achieving one's own identity. To achieve this, all infants need the unqualified, loving acceptance and nurturance from their parents.

Based on "The Child Meets the World," by Antonia Wenkart, Chapter 10 in The Child's Discovery of Himself, *edited by Clark Moustakas. New York: Ballantine Books, 1974.*

Transitions in Early Childhood

Although all children grow in continuous and dynamic ways, every child is different. The process of growth involves several progressive stages of development. Parental awareness of the child's needs at each stage will facilitate and insure a more successful transition from one stage to another. Each level provides parents with an opportunity to stimulate and encourage the child to achieve appropriate mastery of the tasks he faces. No two children will master these tasks at the same chronological age, but in general development will progress along fairly predictable stages.

Birth to Three Months

Contrary to popular belief, the newborn is neither passive nor totally helpless. He can hear, see, smell, and feel shortly after birth, and within a few days his taste buds are activated. He begins to coordinate these senses through seemingly spontaneous and random uncoordinated movements that help him to assimilate and integrate the sensory experience of early life. Infants are responsive to light, sounds, and movement, and begin to focus visual attention to what they hear, feel, and see. The rudiments of sensory motor co-ordination are evident. He is able to give keen attention to objects dangled before his eyes, and attempts to locate sounds by turning his head in their direction. For example, when hearing his mother's voice, he will focus his attention upon her. Thus discrimination between various stimuli begins and expands rapidly. Parents can help by directing the baby's attention to common household items, talking to the baby, making eye contact and naming objects. Appropriate mobiles, cradle gyms, music boxes and other safe articles can be placed within the baby's reach and vision. These provide him with valuable auditory, visual, and tactile stimulation.

Three to Six Months

Random, spontaneous movement now begins to give way to more purposeful reaching out and grasping. The baby is now beginning to discover forms and shapes as well as the feel of hard, soft, and other textures. Rattles of different shapes, colors, and sounds will fascinate him. Toys that are squeezable, multitextured, and colorful, and that he can reach, grasp, release, provide additional tactile and sensory experiences in addition to improving discrimination.

Six to Nine Months

The baby's development is progressing rapidly. He is gaining control over his whole body. He can sit up, control his head movements, and can control his large muscles so that he has some mobility. He is creeping, and sometimes walking, and has a strong desire to touch, manipulate, and put objects in his mouth. Teething is now in full swing, and he tries to chew, bite, or taste anything within his reach not only to relieve the discomfort of teeth pushing their way through his gums, but also to increase his ability to discriminate between different objects and textures. Soft and chewable toys are much appreciated. Small pick-up toys that he can open, turn, close, or spin (particularly multipurpose objects that have moving parts and colorful designs) will be welcome. Bath time now becomes playtime, so a variety of tub toys add fun and interest to this pleasurable experience.

Nine to Twelve Months

The baby is now crawling and walking with some sureness. He is fascinated by the shapes and colors of toys he can push or pull around, such as cars, trucks, or animal figures. These not only keep him company but strengthen muscles as he moves himself and them around the house. The interchange of verbal expressions shared with him during the previous months now become meaningful words. His mental processes are becoming more sophisticated and he begins to understand simple concepts, such as *in, out, full, empty, hard, soft, nice, good, bad,* and so on. Stimulating and amusing toys at this stage include those providing practice in manipulation; stacking; nesting toys and blocks; and those demonstrating cause and effect, such as snap-lock beads and blocks, and those offering an element of surprise, such as jack-in-the-box. Increased mobility enables the child to use toys in new and imaginary ways and in places other than the nursery or playpen.

One to Two Years

This is the energetic, inquisitive, "into everything and everywhere" stage. Walking, grasping, holding, and reaching are done with greater sureness. Toys that give him the opportunity to develop his large muscles and coordination are extremely useful. Ride-on, push and pull, and active games provide good training for these muscles. Even though most toddlers are very active, they are also inquisitive and are able to sit and concentrate on play that stimulates the senses and provides mental exercise. Simple puzzles, take-apart-put-together toys and shape match-ups help hand-eye coordination, increase his concentration span, and sharpen his perception and ability to make comparisons. Rhymes set to music that he can repeat or make on his own, and instruments that make sounds or music provide an outlet to his imagination and imitative skills and assist his body balance.

Blocks (in a variety of shapes) and simple puzzles aid in developing a sense of logic and initial problem-solving skills. Puppets and dolls allow him to act out various emotions that he might not be able to express verbally. This age of exploration requires real paren-

nce. As his loving guide you want him to be safe, nd yet maintain a semblance of order and con-creasing his knowledge and expanding his capacity erful, ever-growing world.

byhood to early childhood. The child may exhibit ssert his emerging personality. The word *no* is a skillful in coordinating his gross and fine motor es, pounding toys, multishaped building blocks, ed. An inexpensive record player will be a source e language and a sense of rhythms. Children of ability to share and interact with others is limited. m a comfortable place in which to use paints and arry-alls are also useful. Miniature housekeeping her kitchen equipment encourage knowledge and ties as well as large muscle development. Small on will strengthen small muscles and stimulate

selves verbally and are more confident and secure eraction is now possible and simple games become his communication skills. He still needs generous and stimulation while he tests himself in the out-ms, throw toys, and games involving other children e has overcome any initial reluctance to participate

d to and/or singing in unison with others. These l music in an unstructured way and prepare them cepts.

ns as he broadens his interests and seeks to under-ssential, but at-home activities may involve a doll urniture. This helps him to translate his understand-ing of what's going on around him. ...all-tales" frequently are encouraged as he plays with doctor kits, dolls, vehicles, and other common objects. Pedal-about vehicles, punching bags, balls, and bean bags all make good exercisers and release energy. The child continues to develop both fine and gross motor skills and muscular control. The rapidity of physical growth begins to level off, and he integrates more skills and strives toward cognitive and intellectual growth. Reading, or being read to, is very important; so too is asking questions and being able to exchange observations and information on a variety of subjects and events.

At five the child may have already been in a preschool or kindergarten program. He may experience personal conflicts in this transition between home and school. This represents his first major separation from his parents and initially may trigger some fear, anxiety, or resistance. Parents need to deal with this with love, praise, reassurance, and firmness. Inspire confidence and interest by continuing school projects at home and by giving extra attention to any area in which your child may need specialized help. Show interest in what he is doing in school and on the playground, but avoid taking over. In helping him to resolve any problem, he may have to understand his input. Help him to seek out alternatives and to decide how he should handle the situation.

Play is the child's work. Toys are his tools. As this work becomes more complex he requires more sophisticated tools to deal with and to comprehend it. Mastering the tasks of each stage of development makes it easier for him to fulfill himself and realize his own potential. He needs parental guidance and understanding to do this.

Based on "Baby: Ages and Stages," by Babs Saoitt. Boston Globe: 24 October 1979.

Meeting 3
Competence vs. Inadequacy

A. Greetings and opening remarks.
1. Participants check off attendance sheet.
2. Leader briefly summarizes the previous meeting.
3. Leader cites handouts and comments appropriately on them.
4. Leader invites comments and questions; initiates short discussion.

B. Topical presentation: The emergence of competence vs. inadequacy—the "me do stage."

C. Discussion highlights.
1. Continue to emphasize the role of feelings as they relate to all learning.
2. Self-discovery emerges from a deep sense of security and trust.
3. Separateness motivates mobility, and combined with greater physical capacities leads to exploration of the child's environment.
4. Mastery of new skills leads to pride and develops a feeling of competence and sense of self.
5. With dyslexic children the messages transmitted by their brain often become garbled and confused. They process oral and written information with less speed, and they therefore need more patience and understanding from parents.
6. Awareness of smallness and dependency incites fear.
7. The child needs limits and structure to protect himself from inexperience and impulses—discipline begins!
8. Separateness and independence involve risk; this is a contradictory concept that is difficult to master, but it explains unrealistic fears.
9. This stage initiates the super-ego; parents say, "No, don't touch."
10. Competency facilitates differentiation, organization, and socialization.
11. Unidentified learning difficulties often bring about frustration and emotional problems. These children need a more tactile and multisensory approach!
12. Other fears are due to lack of experience and initial lack of competence. The child fears the unknown as well as his own fantasies.

D. Human relations training.
1. The leader cites relevant research.
2. Sample lead statements to stimulate discussion:
   a. "You seem to be puzzled about _____ ?"

     b.   "Why do children of this age say 'no' to everything?"
     c.   "What is your experience—can you tell us how you handled _____ ?"
     d.   "What could you have done or said?"
     e.   "How do you think the child was feeling? What was his goal?"
     f.   "What were your reasons for reacting that way?"
     g.   "What alternative do you have for that?"
     h.   "Could you have responded differently?"

   3. Leader may wish to initiate role-playing at this point by inviting parents to play the role of the child, based on a recent interaction between them.

E.   Preparation for the next meeting.
   1. Leader distributes handouts to parents with appropriate comments.
   2. Parents are asked to be ready to present a description of some interaction between themselves and their child.

F.   Suggested parent handouts for meeting 4.
   1. Autonomy vs. Shame and Doubt
   2. Antecedents of Self-Concept
   3. Differences between Children and Adults
   4. The Basic Needs of All Children
   5. Fears
   6. What to Tell Your Children about Santa Claus
   7. Discipline
   8. Helping Children to Deal with Death and Loss

Background for topical presentation: Once the baby is secure in his attachment to his parents, has learned to trust them, others, and himself—he is free to discover his own uniqueness as a human being. Physically he has more than doubled in size and is willing and eager to explore the world around him. He has developed mobility, the rudiments of language, and has learned to get and to give. He wants to learn, to know, and to do, and seeks constant positive feedback. Often known as the "terrible twos," this is the age of exploration and explanation. He is finding out about the environment and the people in it; he is testing his physical capacities and orienting himself in time and space. Up–down, top–bottom, under–over, heavy–light, good–bad, and yes–no are all developing concepts that challenge his physical skills and mental capacities. The child begins to realize himself as a separate person and the fact of his relative smallness. This awareness offers both exhilaration and fear. His new skills and growing competency delight him, yet there is the realization that separateness involves risks, and he is besieged by fear. Even as he demands "to do it by himself" the child still values the limits and security provided by his parents.

Exploration, learning "to do," and knowing about things all lay the groundwork for socialization and the acknowledgment of others. The child is differentiating people and relationships, family from friends, and adults from children. He learns little games, delights in opening and closing things, sings little songs, and as his language skills improve his frustration tolerance grows. Though not ready for interactive play, this is indeed the age of discovery in every sense of the word.

Note: Selma Fraiberg's *The Magic Years* has a good chapter on children's fears.

Competence vs. Inadequacy

The average two-year-old is usually quite active. It is almost imperative that the prudent parent remove every breakable object beyond her reach. She is everywhere at once—touching, squeezing, banging, pulling things out of drawers and cabinets and shelves, exploring and examining with her eyes, hands, and mouth. When denied these activities, she will scream with abandon. When pleased, she rolls on the floor with delight. Her movements are random, uncontrolled, and usually excessive. She cannot drink her milk without spilling or breaking something. Her attention is brief, her aims and goals are constantly changing, and her belongings are scattered throughout the house. She is usually clumsy, unfocused, and inefficient in almost everything she does. She uses her whole body when one hand would do. Yet she wants to do everything from eating to washing herself to dressing. "Me do" is her theme song: "Me eat, me dress, me wipe, me help." Her mispronounced words and inappropriate remarks are often hilarious. To her parents, she is a joy, a delight, but often totally exhausting.

This stage initiates the development of competency. If the child is allowed to "feed" herself, despite the mess she makes or the fact that her food intake decreases; if she is allowed to "put on" her clothes no matter how clumsy she is, or how slowly she does it; if she is encouraged to explore, to climb, to test things out within the limits of safety, then she soon learns that she really can do things by herself and that she is not helpless. Though she still wants to be the center of attention and does not like to share, she is striving to feel more powerful and competent in acting upon her environment.

Normal development entails learning to control one's body and focusing one's attention in order to reduce random and undirected movement. The child learns this by "doing things." The young child is starting to become aware of herself as a person who occupies a distinct personal space and has a precious individuality. Random actions soon become coordinated and efficient when she learns which body parts to use for which task. By separating out the function of parts she not only becomes aware of the limits of her whole body but begins to develop physical motor skills. A baby's first big sorting job is separating herself out as an individual being from all those around her. At first, she tends to see everything as an extension of herself, and then she begins to see people and objects as separate from herself.

Maturity is achieved by separating out the parts from a whole, differentiating them, and then integrating them back into a unity that is understandable and usable. This produces organization. The child must know each of her body parts, where they are, and what they can do before she can coordinate and use them together smoothly. Only when she can differentiate, integrate, and coordinate them together can she achieve usable physical skills and freedom of action, such as washing, talking, reaching, running, and climbing.

This process of identifying differences and similarities in the things around her and then pulling them together is the very core of growth, and gives real meaning to life. This is the preschooler's very serious business. Through play she is organizing and giving meaning to her environment. The parent who discourages, disapproves, or makes the child feel this is "wrong," is encouraging a sense of helplessness and prolonging the child's immaturity.

Tasks of the Toddler: Psychological and Behavioral Characteristics

A. The child reaches a physiological plateau; integrates and refines gross and fine motor activity; toilet training starts.
   1. Gratification from exercise or neuromotor skills.
   2. Play is investigative, imitative, and imaginative.
B. The child differentiates self and begins to develop some control over his impulses (beginning of autonomy).
   1. Exercises body autonomy (sphincter control, eating).
C. Tolerates separation from mother.
   1. Feelings dependent on mother—fears separation.
   2. Behavior identification with parents, siblings, and peers (imitative).
   3. Ambivalent about dependence and independence.
D. Child develops understanding of various concepts and "ethical values," for example, no, good, bad, kind, and nice.
   1. Beginning of conscience—the child is aware of his or her own motives.
   2. Internalized standards of bad–good, right–wrong, and the "beginning of reality testing."
E. The child masters instinctual psychological impulses (oedipal, sexual, and guilt and shame).
   1. Intense feelings; shame, guilt, joy, love, desire to please.
F. The child assimilates (takes in) and handles socialization, acculturation, aggression, and feelings.
   1. Actions somewhat modulated by thought; memory good; animistic and original thinking.
   2. Learns speech, communication improves and expands.
G. Learns sex distinction.
   1. Broader sex curiosity; differentiation.
   2. Questions about birth, death, and the like begin.

Peer Group Socialization and Play

The two-year-old has a limited tolerance for group relationships. She is more comfortable with one or two others for part of the time each day. However, by the time she is around three she can cope more easily with a group of several peers and with one or two adults for approximately three to six hours a day outside her home. At first she may experience separation anxiety, or the parents may feel this quite acutely, because entrance to nursery school marks another milestone along the road to independence.

Peer group association is important because it provides many learning opportunities—for example, how to respond to another adult; how to become a member of a group; how to become a leader; how to deal with approval and disapproval from others; and how to understand the feelings of others. Most groups are motivated by play activities. One learns how to share, to obey rules, to take defeat. Play materials are often more abundant and more varied in a group. The importance of guided play needs a special emphasis, because there is much evidence that later school learning in academic subjects like reading, writing, and mathematics is based on the kind of experience a child has in the preschool years.

Play that involves the use of small muscles favors writing development. Games that make use of symbols are a foundation for learning to read. Crawling, climbing, and running help coordination. Large muscle use in body movement helps the child get a feeling of self in mastery of situations, as well as of her own body parts. Play in making music gives one the feeling of rhythm as well as the pleasure of doing something successfully with others. Stimulation of all sense organs aids perception and the capacity to use alternate and composite ways of learning. All of these play experiences enable the child to increase her physical flexibility and her ability to perceive, cope, and adapt to the multiple demands of her own needs as well as those of her peers, family, and ultimately her community and society.

Deprivation of the use of large and small muscles in infancy and the preschool period affects the emotional development of the child. If prolonged, such movement restriction has profound effects in later life. An abnormal mobility pattern, as detected by a developmental examination, is an important sign of either a physical injury or of an emotional deprivation in the past. A child whose activity is restricted by a cast, splints, or traction should be given substitute experiences. If a child cannot run, climb, or cling, her hands should have other choices as in self-feeding, squeezing balls, playing with clay, throwing objects, tearing paper, and crayoning. It is extremely important that children with physical limitations or illnesses be provided with adequate compensatory activities in order that their gross and fine motor skills, as well as their social development, proceed in as normal a fashion as possible.

THE TODDLER AND
THE PRESCHOOL AGE

As the preschool-age child achieves autonomy he gains a sense of "selfhood" that gives him a feeling of self-control over his body functions and initiates independence from his parents. This new stage also prepares him for greater socialization.

The child's progress toward "selfhood" is often met with ambivalence by both parents and child. The parents' temporary wish for the continuing dependence of the child and the inner developmental thrust for independence on the part of the child often account for the clash of wills over such matters as eating, sleeping and toileting. The parents often find this stage disconcerting, but as they gradually realize its importance they allow the child some control over his actions.

The toddler is often upset and confused by the negative reaction of his parents when he accomplishes something he thought would meet with their approval or had formerly been approved without objection. He is puzzled by their angry reactions to his messiness and to little accidents that they had once accepted or ignored. These reactions and their new expectations puzzle him because his development is dictated by his inner time clock. Thus he tests conditions and people constantly. He is not as assertive or as sure of himself as his parents expect, yet he is often too bold and aggressive to suit them. He indulges in fantasies that adults consider humorous. Yet, when he shares purely imaginary activities with them, they regard him as not being truthful. Parents must realize that the child's use of imagination is a way of testing reality.

During the preschool period, play is the child's work and his principal medium for learning. The child's curiosity abounds with interest and eagerness to explore, learn, and try new things. He is keen and perceptive and wants to feel, explore, and understand the world of things and people. His language is expanding, and he derives great pleasure from learning the names of people, objects, and places. He loves songs and rhymes and delights in echoing words just for the effect they have on his parents and other adults. Cognition flourishes particularly when his parents and teachers are encouraging. This sets the foundations for cognitive and social learning and prepares the child for moral and ethical training.

Parents who actively help their child to cope and manage his feelings and behavior are encouraging him to become more sensitive, confident, and secure. Problems common to this stage concern sexual identity, socialization with peer group, managing feelings, reality, fantasy, aggression, and the emergence of conscience.

Based on Problems in Child Behavior and Development, *by M.J. Senn and Albert J. Solnit. Philadelphia: Lea & Febiger, 1968.*

What Children Should Know
before Entering School

Most school-age children usually possess some basic skills, taught in the home, that are indicative of their readiness for the school experience. Those children who are not able to perform most of the following tasks are likely to fail in school, will have difficulties in getting along with peers, and will generally be unhappy.

1. *Dressing habits.* The child should be able to dress with minimal help; be able to put on, as well as remove, outer clothing and boots. Can button and use zippers or other fasteners. Can recognize own clothing and place it on a hook or other assigned place.

2. *Toilet habits.* Able to use handkerchief or tissues. Does not drool or make unnecessary sounds. Able to wash face and hands. Cares for self at toilet. Does not wet or soil clothing.

3. *Eating habits.* Can get a drink and handle a glass or a cup by herself. Can feed herself and use basic utensils, as well as napkin; has a diversified diet and can adjust to new food or a new food schedule.

4. *Adjusting to being away from parent(s).* Is able to separate from parents without undue anxiety. Able to control fears when parents leave. Is able to tolerate other children and involve herself without overreacting or being excessively dependent upon the teacher or other children. Can remain in school for at least two to three hours without undue tears. Moves toward other children and can play happily with them. Can go out of her home, her yard, and immediate neighborhood successfully on her own.

5. *Play skills.* Walks up and down stairs unassisted. Can hop on one foot and can run. Is able to roll a ball on the floor back and forth to another person. Is able to throw and sometimes catch a ball. Understands and follows simple directions and ideas about space and motion. Plays reasonably well with children of similar ages. Adjusts herself to new playmates, in addition to familiar ones and family members. Adjusts herself to new games or rules. Does not fear other children and is generally not teased by them. Does not hurt or purposefully injure other children. Generally has a good disposition.

6. *Communication skills.* Is able to speak using short, easy sentences. Speech contains little or no baby talk. Knows how to ask for things she wants instead of crying or pointing at them. Is free from gross speech defects.

7. *Attention skills.* Is able to listen to and enjoy a short story read to her in a group. Can give her attention to a play project or to simple directions when performing an activity. Can sit reasonably quiet for periods of ten minutes or longer. Has some attention span.

8. *Cutting, coloring, and art skills.* Enjoys using crayons or chalk. Can draw a form that is recognizable. Can fill in or color outlined figures. Able to identify and match some primary colors. Notices and identifies colors of clothes and things. Can use paper or blackboard. Can cut with blunt scissors and use simple tools successfully.

9. *Number and form skills.* Differentiates between big and little, between one and two things, more than or less than, and is able to bring two things, three things, and so on, on request. Is able to fit blocks and toys together and loves jigsaw puzzles. Learns differences between things that are round, square, octagonal, and so on; that a table has corners, a tree is tall, and other similar ideas.

When a child is immature or has other problems, schoolwork is a mental strain rather than a challenge. She is apt to develop nervous habits or emotional blocks that can prevent learning.

Parents should avoid forcing children into any task until they are mature enough or ready to learn it. Mastery of tasks depends upon physical, social, and emotional maturity as well as on the encouragement and example provided by the parents and the experiences she gains through daily tasks, which are basic to school readiness!

CHILDHOOD SEXUALITY

Infancy and early childhood possess erotic pleasures of their own kind. Erections of the penis are common to boys of any age, and are manifested in the neonatal period. Some parents inadvertently stimulate by diapering too tightly, or by overcleaning and rubbing the genitals. The baby or toddler does not possess thought processes as adults know them, but he is beginning to have awareness of sex differences and ways of obtaining sexual pleasure. He is consciously or unconsciously driven to gratify himself by fantasies, masturbation, and sex play. It is abhorrent for some parents to realize that children under five years of age find genital stimulation a source of interest, excitement, comfort, and pleasure.

The anxiety felt by the parents can result in shame and guilt in the child. There is good clinical evidence that extreme censure of sex explorations, as of other learning early in life, creates conflicts and inhibitions if sustained for even a short time. The child becomes morally "good" but at a price paid not so much in early childhood but in later childhood and especially adolescence and in the adult years. The sexual pleasure of intercourse is based not only on the physical contacts and physiological processes involved, but equally on the fantasy and sensuous thoughts that precede, accompany, and follow orgasm. These have their origin in the attitudes and experiences of parents and children long before adult sexuality is established. The experiences of early life are buried deeply, become unconscious, but are influential in deciding the patterns of reacting to life situations, to peers, to authority figures, and to sex drives.

Parents need to accept their young child's curiosity as physiologically and psychologically normal. Such behavior is not necessarily indicative of precocious sex development or a life of perversion. Sex curiosity and sex play are important learning experiences and should not be confused with morality. Parents should tactfully guide the child into socially acceptable behavior by distraction and substitute opportunities, instead of censure and indignation. At this period the child is impressionable and very concerned with the reaction of his parents. Parents should help the child understand that sexual play is not socially acceptable in public, but they must be careful not to make the child ashamed of his feelings.

The preschool period is an important one for sex education, not by verbal instruction but in the way that parents tolerate their child's activities, listen to questions, and give him honest answers that he can understand.

As in all learning the child begins with himself, with what comes natural, with what motivates him. He learns what he is ready to learn at the time he is ready to learn it. In part this is decided by his earlier expressions and the phase of development he has approached.

This period is not appropriate for formal lessons on the sexual nature of life, or for parents' exposing themselves in the nude to help the child accept sex difference. Commonly this leads to harmful overstimulation rather than healthy learning. Taking children to bed in the name of comforting the child is not advised. Prudish modesty or nonchalant exhibitionism on the part of the parents should be avoided.

It is common for boys to worry about genital function and its difference from that of girls. Girls also make comparisons and fear the worst. Anatomical differences are difficult to comprehend, and one of childhoods' recurrent fantasies deals with genital injury. Manipulation of genitals and anus must be kept to a minimum.

THE DEVELOPMENT OF ATTITUDES

The development of the concept of "self" or of "me" as an entity is a process that evolves slowly. It obviously includes the physical body, the parts of which are slowly differentiated and named by the child. Hence as the child matures he can identify his arms, legs, head, feet, hands, and so forth. This process of identification is enhanced by the acquisition of language, which his parents are eager to impart beginning at birth. Language is a system of significant symbols that denotes not only objects, places, and people but also thoughts, feelings, and ways of behaving and doing. Thus, early on, parents convey to their child their ideas of propriety and ways of behaving and doing on both a conscious and unconscious level.

Their approval or disapproval of what he does or does not do, their attitude toward themselves and others, and their manner of enforcing rules before the child even knows the meaning of rules, are all subtly but unmistakably conveyed to the young child. The parents' aspirations for his success in school, active participation with peers, and choice of career are unconsciously transmitted to the child. His ideas and priorities are engendered as parents assume the attitudes of their society and insist upon his conformance.

Thus the young child absorbs and internalizes the rules and values as defined by contemporary society as a matter of course.

Very early, parents use simplified language such as "no-no, mustn't touch, no good, not nice" as symbols of prohibition. The child will test these constantly under various conditions but will gradually realize that he must must stop, withdraw, or ignore a variety of events, objects, and situations if the "self" he is becoming is to enjoy approval. In acquiring the significance and meaning of these various prohibitions (as well as those of approval) the child also acquires the parental attitudes associated with the behaviors in question. Thus admonitions become warnings of danger, disapproval, and rejection, while approvals represent acceptance, caring, and love.

Thus the acquisition of meaning via parental admonitions is both positive and negative. The child acquires his parents' attitudes toward the behaviors in question. The emotional overtones, facial expressions, and the immediacy with which parents react become imbedded in the child's understanding. In time he will use the same verbal symbols and attitudes that were used by the parents. For example, it is quite normal to see a toddler standing before a stove or television and reaching one hand toward the dial, and then stopping to slap the offending hand with the other and saying "no, no, mustn't touch!" Thus, he is stimulating himself to initiate the appropriate response expected by his parents. The child internalizes the parental rules and actions toward himself in the way his parents have acted toward him. His sense of other versus self assists his differentiation of himself from his parents. It also promotes the sharing and meaning of symbols with others and implies mutual role taking.

Based on "The Child Meets the World," by Antonia Wenkart. Chapter 10 in The Child's Discovery of Himself, *edited by Clark Moustakas. New York: Ballantine Books, 1974.*

Meeting 4
Autonomy vs. Shame and Doubt

A. Greetings and opening remarks.
   1. Leader continues the pattern of checking attendance, summarizing the previous meeting, and discussing handouts.
   2. Leader requests volunteers to describe verbal interaction between parent and child.
   3. Leader explains role-playing.
   4. Volunteers may role-play reported incidents.
   5. Leader compliments participants and guides their performance.
B. Topical presentation: Autonomy vs. shame and doubt.
   1. Presentations continue to be given in open-ended fashion; parents may interrupt with questions and comments at any time.
C. Discussion highlights.
   1. Self-control and inner directedness are rooted in the development of autonomy.
   2. Child needs to feel that she has some say over what happens to her in order to commit herself to any task or any person.
   3. Child is still exploring her environment; toilet flushing is difficult to comprehend and often incites fear.
   4. Fears are rooted in sense of helplessness and lack of control.
   5. Parent takeover of this task usually leads to lack of motivation later on or other emotional problems.
   6. Parents should not compare child with others or force toilet training.
   7. Parents should understand fears in the context of the child's development and relative maturity. They should never make her ashamed or destroy her self-esteem.
   8. Parents should handle toilet training according to child's readiness; they must always be careful and sensitive to her feelings.
   9. Discipline provides the structure and security that are basic to the child's need for trust, competence, and autonomy.
   10. Discipline teaches impulse control and social awareness. It is the foundation for the super-ego.
D. Human relations training.
   1. Leader now handles questions by pointing out the dynamics involved, and responds to the feelings.
   2. Helps parent to sort out alternatives and come to a reasonable solution.

3. Zeroes in on what the child is feeling.
4. Sample lead questions to stimulate discussion:
    a.   "You felt anxious about _____ ?"
    b.   "How did you feel when your relatives were pressuring you?"
    c.   "How do you think your child felt?"
    d.   "You feel puzzled that she flushes the toilet on her own but will not go—can you think why she would do this?"
    e.   "What were your options when you punished the child?"
E. Preparation for next meeting.
    1. Distribute handouts.
F. Suggested parent handouts for meeting 5.
    1. TV's Influence on Children
    2. Rules for Keeping Poisons and Children Apart
    3. Responding to Children's Sexuality
    4. Some Reasons for Poor Eating Habits
    5. Characteristics of Young School-Age Children

Background for topical presentation: Between the ages of two-and-a-half to four years most parents initiate toilet training. During this period the child becomes aware of holding on and letting go—which is generally indicated by the maturation of her sphincter muscle. When allowed to perform this in accordance to the development of her inner time schedule the child learns to regulate her behavior and to gain control over her movements and later over her impulses. This helps her to develop confidence in her own ability to progress further. (Girls typically develop approximately six to twelve months earlier than boys.)

When the parent insists on taking over this control, however, the child tends to either "hold on" or to withdraw, and emotionally develops the feeling that she has little or no control over what happens to her. Excessive holding on can result in encopresis and emotional problems, which accentuate the clash of wills between parent and child. This may produce a child who lacks motivation; is rigid; compulsive; unable to make decisions; who lacks flexibility, and is generally apathetic or indifferent, particularly in matters that are important to her parents. Still other possible characteristics might include inner hostility and lack of spontaneity, as well as various types of fears.

Autonomy vs. Shame and Doubt

Stage three usually spans the second and third years of life, the period that Freudian theory calls the anal stage. Erikson sees this as a time when autonomy begins. He explains this as an inner feeling or a sense of control over what happens to the child. This new dimension builds upon the child's emerging motor and mental abilities. At this stage the child not only can walk, but she also can climb, open and close things, drop, push, pull, hold on, and let go. The child takes pride in these new accomplishments and demonstrates that she wants to do more and more by herself, such as pulling the wrapper off a piece of candy, feeding herself, selecting the vitamin out of the bottle, or flushing the toilet. When parents recognize the young child's need to do those things that she is capable of doing at her own pace through control of her muscles, impulses, herself and, more importantly, her environment—she can then begin to acquire a sense of autonomy or inner control.

However, when her caretakers are impatient, or are insensitive to this need and do for her what she is capable of doing for herself, they are reinforcing a sense of shame and doubt. In a sense they are implying that the child is "not able" to do anything for herself. To be sure, every parent has rushed his child at times due to other pressures. Children are hardy enough to endure occasional lapses of sensitivity when parents take over! It is only when caretaking is consistently overprotective, and criticism of "accidents" (whether these be wetting, soiling, spilling, or breaking things) is harsh and unthinking, that the child develops an excessive sense of shame with respect to other people, and an excessive sense of doubt about her own abilities to control her world and most importantly of all, *herself.*

If the child goes through this stage with less autonomy than shame or doubt, she will be handicapped in her attempts to achieve autonomy at adolescence and even in adulthood. Contrariwise, the child who moves through this stage with her sense of autonomy buoyantly outbalancing her feelings of shame and doubt will be well on her way to becoming autonomous at later phases of her life. However, the balance of autonomy to shame and doubt set up during this period is subject to change in either a positive or negative direction by subsequent events and experiences.

In addition, if too much autonomy is allowed before the child can handle it, feelings of anxiety and insecurity can result. Lack of limits may cause the child to feel that she can dominate her parents into submission to do her will. At the same time, this enormous power will cause her to become tyrannical, while inwardly becoming fearful and anxious because she can no longer depend upon the structure and limits usually set by her parents, who essentially are the bedrock of her emotional security. When parents become aware of this and confidently take over over their role, the child is really eager to give it up in exchange for the comfort and security that their support provides. Therefore, helping the child to develop a healthy sense of autonomy, or inner control over her instinctual and usually self-defeating impulses, in no way implies that she should control her parents. On the contrary, it means that the child learns to identify and trust her own feelings in terms of what *is or is not appropriate.* Her parents still need to provide the structure, limits, and guidance whereby she gradually develops decision-making skills over her life situations. Eventually, this helps her to realize herself and her potential, and to learn to make independent decisions.

Based on "Erik Erikson's Eight Ages of Man," by David Elkind, New York Times Magazine, *5 April 1970.*

ANTECEDENTS OF SELF-CONCEPT

Dr. Harry Stack Sullivan viewed the child's sense of self as evolving gradually during the *first year* of life, primarily as a consequence of the ministration of the person who takes care of the child. If the person is loving, comforting, and meets the infant's needs, the infant generalizes a feeling of "good me." On the other hand, if the caretaker is anxious, tense, and rejecting, this is communicated to the infant, who experiences a generalized feeling of "bad me," and if it continues to the extreme, it can be interpreted as "not me." Sullivan calls this *empathy*. This is not particularly mysterious since most of us communicate through empathy. When we note that a tense, fidgety person "makes me nervous," we are talking about empathy.

The importance of a general sense of "good me" to the infant has now been well documented. Infants need to be mothered, held, rocked, touched, and talked to daily if normal development is to occur. The mere meeting of physical needs (for example, nutrition) is not enough. In the absence of adequate mothering or the presence of a pervasive sense of "bad me," some infants withdraw and become apathetic and listless. If ignored to the point of "not me" they literally shrivel up and die, while others become permanently impaired, both emotionally and intellectually.

With the development of speech at about age two, the child enters into the era of what Sullivan called childhood (what is today called early childhood—from two to five). Language opens up a wide range of potential for defining the self-concept, which now can be affected by verbal appraisals of approval and disapproval, of affection and rejection. The quality of the child's self-concept will be determined by his perception of approval and disapproval in his experience.

As an example, Sullivan describes what he called the "malevolent" child. Such a child, because of rejecting or bitter parents, may have received a preponderance of negative appraisals: "Can't you do anything right?" "Oh, you are so clumsy!" "Why do you always look like a rag doll?" and "Leave me alone." While the youngster may have had some good self-appraisals as well, these have been "disassociated," or dropped from his awareness. Thus they play a lesser part in his interpersonal dealings than do the overwhelming negative appraisals.

In his need for security, the "malevolent" child sees in others primarily what he sees in himself. Accordingly, a child of this sort will see only the negative aspects of a person, even when that person is kind and interested in helping him. People who may try to be friendly to a withdrawn child are often discouraged because they can be attacked in a most vicious way. The child, through the microscope of his negative self-concept, seeks out and finds the negative aspects of the helping person's behavior and ignores the rest. It's almost as if in so doing the child restores his feeling of being human by finding that others are as bad as he feels himself to be.

Sullivan felt that the "juvenile" era, roughly from five to ten, offers new opportunities for the strengthening of the self-concept. The child is now in school and has a new opportunity to incorporate the appraisals of teachers and other adults into his self-concept. Also, as he engages in group activities with his peers and is involved in competition and collaboration with them, he begins to incorporate their evaluations. In Sullivan's view, the self-concept is never static, and the negative self-image inculcated by rejecting parents can, with the consistent help of patient teachers and peers, sometimes be subordinate to a positive self-concept. Unfortunately, the reverse can also be true, and lifelong negative self-appraisals can be acquired from peers and teachers during this era.

Very distressing and widespread evidence of what often happens to the child's self-concept during this period is shown by the slow reader. For whatever reason, the child who is not reading by the end of first grade begins to feel that he is a "flop" in life. More and more, failure to read has become associated with negative self-appraisal. Very soon anything connected with reading begins to arouse anxiety. So, to protect himself from embarrassment, the child avoids reading. Such avoidance only complicates his problem, because it makes further progress in reading impossible. To really help such children, the major task is not solely to teach them to read but to help them to refurbish or build up their self-concept. The latter is indeed difficult without parental help.

Excerpts from " 'Good Me' or 'Bad Me'—The Sullivan Approach to Personality," by David Elkind, New York Times Magazine, *24 September 1972.*

Differences between
Children and Adults

The psychological functioning of adults has been established and proceeds along fixed lines. They are generally in touch with their feelings and motives for acting as they do. Their habits are fixed, and their modes of operating are fairly predictable.

Children are constantly changing from one stage to another. Initially totally dependent, they respond to inner needs. Gradually, as they become more secure and are able to move on to being more independent, they are able to react to the environmental stimuli. In this process they are not always predictable. What they valued at three may be considered utterly useless or rejected at nine. Their feelings and attitudes are in constant flux as they grow in understanding and experience. Therefore, parents need to interpret behavior according to the child's level of development.

Adults measure the passing of time by clocks and calendars.

Children's sense of time is based on the urgency of instinctual and emotional needs. Initially children often confuse night and day. They have a marked intolerance for postponement. The child is not aware nor does she understand "tomorrow" or "in a little while." She responds to the inner needs of the present. If she is hungry she needs to gratify the pain of hunger. If she needs affection, she is not able to comprehend that she has to wait until her parents return from work. Her frustration tolerance is low and she has an intense sensitivity to the length of separations from her security base, that is, her parents. Children find it difficult to deal with tomorrow or with the future because their experiences are so limited and their sense of time is just developing.

Adults interpret events and daily occurrences in the realistic perspective of their own experience.

Children respond to events in a totally egocentric manner—or how they directly affect them. For example, the adult may change residence because the growth in family members realistically requires more rooms. The child may perceive this same change solely with reference to herself. For example, she may perceive it as a loss of her old friends; or she may perceive the birth of a new baby as a hostile act on the part of her parents toward her—that is, as a rejection of her.

Adults are generally experienced enough (and due to their reason and intellect) are better able to deal with life's inconsistencies or unexplainable events.

Children's behavior is often governed by their primitive wishes and impulses or the more irrational parts of their mind. Any threat to their emotional security is responded to with great anxiety, denial, distortion of reality, reversal, or displacement of feelings. Such reactions do not help them to cope or deal with the situation, but instead put them at the mercy of events.

For example, when there is parental discord children generally feel guilty because they feel they have caused this strife. Thus, they place on themselves the anger they may feel toward their parents because of the insecurity created by their perception of an impending break-up. They are in conflict between fear of loss and the deep attachment they feel toward both parents. This increases their insecurity.

THE BASIC NEEDS
OF ALL CHILDREN

Children need:

1. Care and mothering to mature normally with unbroken continuity of affectionate and stimulating relationships.
2. Body needs nourished and protected.
3. Intellect needs to be stimulated.
4. Interaction with adults.

Children are different from adults whose functioning proceeds on fixed lines:

1. Children change constantly from one state of growth to another, and their needs for parenting or independence change accordingly.
2. Children have their own built-in time sense based on the urgency of instinctual and emotional needs. This results in marked intolerance for postponement of gratification and frustration and an intense sensitivity to the length of separation. Adults measure the passing of time by the clock and calendar.
3. Young children experience events in an egocentric manner, that is, as happening solely with reference to their own persons. A child may see a residential move as a personal loss solely imposed on him. He may see the birth of a sibling as a hostile act on the part of the parents. Adults see events in a more realistic perspective.
4. Children are governed and function by the irrational parts of their minds, that is, primitive wishes and impulses. Consequently, they respond to any threat to their emotional security with fantastic anxieties, denial or distortion of reality, reversal or displacement of feelings—reactions that are no help for coping but rather put them at the mercy of events. Adults are generally better able to deal with the vagaries of life via reason and interaction.
5. Children lack the capacity for maintaining positive emotional ties with a number of different individuals. They will freely love more than one adult *only* if the individuals

in question feel positively toward one another. Failing this, they become prey to severe and crippling loyalty conflicts.

6.   Children have no psychological conception of relationship by blood tie until quite late in their development. What registers in their minds are the day-to-day interchanges with caring adults who, on the strength of this, become the parent figure they become attached to.

The parent who daily provides comfort, nourishment, affection, and stimulation becomes the "psychological parent" in whose care the child can feel valued and wanted. An absent biological parent will remain or become a stranger to the young child.

Legislative bodies and courts should give the child "party-status," the right to be represented by counsel in any contested placement.

By and large, society must use each child's placement as an occasion for protecting future generations of children by increasing the number of adults-to-be who are likely to be adequate parents. Only in the implementation of this policy does there lie a real opportunity to break the cycle of sickness and hardship bequeathed from one generation to the next by adults who, as children, were denied the least detrimental alternatives.

Based on "Beyond the Best Interest of the Child," by J. Goldstein, Ann Frued, A.J. Solnit, New York: The Free Press, 1973.

FEARS

Into any child's life can come frightening and unhappy incidents that set up special fears, and you as parents naturally do your best to protect your child from such especially frightening incidents.

But you cannot protect her from all fears. As the child grows up, she seems to need to go through a series of fears that appear and then later disappear. Each child differs somewhat but in general, each age seems to bring its own characteristic fears. A much abbreviated summary of some of the most outstanding fears that are likely to develop in almost any child, from age to age, is as follows.

Two Years

- Many fears, chiefly auditory, such as trains, trucks, thunder, flushing of toilet, and vacuum cleaner.
- Visual fears: dark colors, large objects, trains, or hats.
- Spatial fears: toy or crib moved from usual place; moving to a new house; fear of going down the drain.
- Personal fears: mother's departure, or separation from her at bedtime. Rain and wind.

Two-and-a-half Years

- Many fears, especially spatial: fear of movement or of having objects moved.
- Any different orientation, as someone entering house by a different door.
- Large objects, such as trucks, approaching.

Four Years

- Auditory fears again, especially fire engines.
- The dark.
- Wild animals.
- Mother leaving, especially going out at night.

Five Years

- Not a fearful age. More visual fears than others.
- Less fear of animals, bad people, or bogeyman.
- Concrete, down-to-earth fears: bodily harm, falling, dogs.
- The dark.
- That mother will not return.

Six Years

- Very fearful. Especially auditory fears: doorbell, telephone, static, ugly voice tones, flushing of toilet, insect, and bird noises.
- Fear of supernatural: ghosts, witches.
- Fear that someone is hiding under the bed.
- Spatial fears: fear of being lost, fear of the woods.
- Fear of the elements: fire, water, thunder, lightning.
- Fear of sleeping alone in a room or of being the only person on a floor of the house.
- Fear that mother will not be home when the child arrives home, or that something will happen to her or that she may die.
- Afraid others will hit her.
- Brave about big hurts but fears splinters, little cuts, blood, or nose drops.

Seven Years

- Many fears, especially visual: the dark, attics, cellars.
- Interprets shadows as ghosts and witches.
- Fears war, spies, burglars, or people hiding in closet or under bed.
- Fears now stimulated by reading, radio, TV, or movies.
- Worries about things: not being liked, being late to school.

Eight and Nine Years

- Fewer fears and less worrying. No longer fears the water. Less fear of the dark. Good evaluation, and fears are reasonable: about personal inability and failure, especially school failure.

Ten Years

- Many fears, though fewer than at the ages which immediately follow. Animals, especially snakes and wild animals, are things most feared. The dark is feared by a few. Also high places, fires, and criminals, "killers," or burglars.

- A few are beginning spontaneously to mention things they are not afraid of: chiefly the dark, dogs, or being left alone.

Studies of thousands of normal children have shown us that as any child matures, she is likely from time to time to exhibit fears of things that often seem to her parents to be quite harmless. However—and this should be most reassuring to parents—these fears do not appear completely at random, nor are they different for every child.

On the contrary, it is known they appear, and soon disappear, in an ordered, patterned fashion that often shows great similarity from child to child. For example, as the preceding list suggests, two-year-olds often fear any sudden loud sounds, like vacuum cleaners or locomotives. Two-and-a-half-year-olds are more likely to have spatial fears, or fears of moving objects. Three-year-olds may most often fear things seen.

What Not to Do When Your Child Is Afraid

- Don't ever make fun of her fears.
- Don't shame her before others because of her fears.
- Don't force her to face the thing she fears before she is ready unless you are very sure you are right to do so. (And you seldom will be.)
- Don't become impatient and treat her as if she were babyish because she is afraid.
- Don't assume that it is necessarily your fault, or her fault, that she is afraid.
- Don't necessarily feel that it is bad or unnatural for the child to have some fears.

What to Do When Your Child Is Afraid

- Respect her fears.
- Realize that she will outgrow most of them.
- Allow her at least a reasonable period of withdrawal from feared things before you attempt to help her adjust to them.

Give her a chance to become used to fearful situations, a little at a time. If she fears great heights, accustom her first to small elevations; if she is afraid of dogs, let her first get acquainted with a puppy. (This gradual approach does not, however, work with all children. Some children need to take the plunge and get it over with.)

When and if she comes to the period of compulsively overapproaching a formerly feared object or situation (her natural method of tackling her fears) help her to have the experience she desires, but under your supervision. If she was first afraid of fires, she may later have a strong desire to set fires and to play with fire. Let her light the fire in the fireplace or the candles for the table. Or let her help burn the trash, or help with a bonfire—of course under your most careful supervision.

Analyze her fears in relation to her personality. Does she characteristically fear strange sounds or sights? Does she fear movement? Try within reason to spare her situations that you know will cause her to be fearful.

Familiarize yourself with the kinds of fears that children naturally experience at different ages. You can take more lightly a fear that is common to the majority of children at some particular age. It will usually not last long.

If your child seems to fear some large, general situation that she must nevertheless experience, as school, analyze the situation to find out what specific aspect of it has caused her fear.

But if your child's fear is excessive and troublesome and you cannot find out the cause, and time does not take care of it, you may wish to seek specialized help in aiding her to solve her problem.

Excerpted from Infant and Child in the Culture of Today, *by Arnold L. Gesell and Frances L. Ilg. Reprinted by permission of Harper & Row, Publishers, Inc.*

WHAT TO TELL YOUR CHILDREN
ABOUT SANTA CLAUS

"There really isn't a Santa Claus, is there, Mummy?" Six-year-old Peter regarded his mother searchingly. Mother hesitated for a moment. She had known that this day would come—but still, questions about Santa, like questions about sex, often pop up when we're not quite prepared for them. She decided to tell the truth. "No, Peter, there really isn't any Santa Claus." "That's what I thought," replies Peter comfortably. "He's just a man dressed up, who goes all over the world and comes down the chimney and gives everybody presents."

Thus, as you can see, most children (for Peter is quite typical of others), do not *find out* about Santa Claus all at once. They take from a skeptical environment only as much as they are ready and able to accept.

Two other six-year-olds, a little further along the road to enlightenment, were overheard by us in the following conversation: Jetty: "Do you think Santa Claus is real?" Timothy: "No." Jetty: "Santa Claus used to be St. Nicholas and then St. Nicholas died, so they just took a man as Santa Claus and put a beard on him."

Perhaps these two anecdotes will help to answer the question: "Should we allow children to believe in Santa Claus?" An inevitable question which we hear every year as Christmastime comes around.

Most families, we find, don't worry about the problem—in fact, they don't even consider it to be a problem. Their youngest children believe in Santa. The older ones don't. And the transition from belief to disbelief is in most cases quite painless.

But every year a few parents worry about what will happen when their children *find out* that there is no Santa. They fear that if the child finds out that something he's been allowed to believe really "isn't so," this will undermine his faith in other things that they tell him.

It is our experience that only the extremely fragile child will be harmed by such a "disillusionment." Certainly thousands, if not millions, of people have believed, and then not believed, and have still been left with a warm spot in their hearts for the whole idea.

Perhaps one of the main reasons why most children are not too much disturbed by the discovery that Santa Claus is not "real" is that, as the preceding anecdotes show, this discovery does not come about all at once. Most children do not believe it the first time that somebody tells them that Santa is not real. They are so far from ready that they probably do not even hear the bad news.

If a child hears that Santa isn't real—when he is very young—he just doesn't "hear" this information because it means nothing to him. Later, when he does "hear" it, it means that he is on the verge of being ready to accept. If he is unhappy and tearful and denies the truth, that too usually means that he is almost ready to accept. Vigorous, tearful denial of some enlightenment usually means that a child is on the verge of being ready to understand and believe the new thing. And even when they do finally hear and can even repeat that there is no Santa Claus, most of them believe only as much as they are ready to believe. This is a comforting thing to know about children—that the human being normally has great powers of self-protection.

Christmas means very little to the extremely young child—or at least usually means something quite different from what his parents have anticipated. Your nine-month-old baby, instead of being delighted with the large wooly dog which you have provided with such expense and anticipation, may merely howl in fright every time the toy is brought near to him.

Your two- or two-and-a-half-year-old, instead of being the little angel you had expected, just sits by greedily and every time a present from the tree is offered to anyone else, selfishly inquires, "Anything more for me? Anything more for me?"

Here, as in all fields of behavior, if we know what is reasonable to expect and do not expect too much, we are less likely to be disappointed.

Many two-year-olds whom we have known are not yet ready for Santa Claus. They either are not interested or may even be frightened by him. The tree is the important thing at two; he gazes at it and its lights starry-eyed. There is also some interest in presents, but not much in the giver.

The three-year-old has grown up a lot. His interest in Santa may be rather vague and he may be a little hazy as to details, but he is interested. And he is usually pleased and excited by the presents he receives.

Four, as a rule, believes in Santa Claus in every detail. And he is deeply interested in every detail.

But five and six are the real Santa Claus ages, when overwhelming interest and great delight and unshakable belief are expressed. The joy which most children experience in Santa Claus at these ages is surely worth any little disillusionment that may come about later.

The average five-year-old has an extremely realistic approach to Santa Claus. He definitely thinks of him as a real man living in a real house and having a real wife. He often makes plans to visit him, and likes to write (or at least dictate) letters to him asking for the things he wants.

Six does the same. The first letters he writes, or prints, may be to Santa with lists of the presents he wants to receive. Most six-year-olds are very firm in their belief about Santa Claus—insistent and emotional. They will often fiercely deny any hint that he is not real.

However, as in many things, this fierce denial may just precede a beginning skepticism. Some six-year-olds and many sevens are at least a little bit skeptical and may deny some aspects of the Santa Claus myth, such as, he comes down the chimney.

A few eight-year-olds still believe, but a good many children at eight, and nearly all by nine, are able to substitute a concept of a spirit of Christmas or a spirit of giving for a purely physical Santa. And most make this substitution with only a few pangs and with little real difficulty.

Dr. Gesell has commented on this subject: "Usually a child can assimilate, adore and in time deny the concept of Santa Claus without suffering any scars of disillusionment."

Excerpted from Infant and Child, *by Arnold L. Gesell and F.L. Ilg. New York: Harper & Row, 1943.*

DISCIPLINE

Discipline is simultaneously the most important and the most difficult responsibility facing parents. Infant behavior is primarily instinctual and motivated by the pleasure principle. As the infant matures, impulsivity begins to yield to more controlled behavior. Eventually behavior becomes more appropriate and the child becomes a social being. In this process of growing, children take their cues and formulate their concepts of the world around them by observing what is important or not important to their parents, or the most significant people to them. Children need to organize and make sense of the bewildering mass of stimuli around them. By use of all their senses they assimilate, differentiate, integrate, identify, and categorize what is good or bad; dangerous or safe; acceptable or unacceptable; happy or sad; lovely or ugly; useful or useless; and so on.

It has been said that the three "E's" of learning are *Example*, *Encouragement*, and *Experience*. Certainly in the process of growing up the examples set by and the encouragement children receive from their parents are of utmost importance. In addition, structure, guidelines, and rules provide children with a sense of dependability and security. At first they imitate the behavior they see. As children develop trust and feel more secure, they begin to feel freer to explore, investigate, experiment, and try out new experiences. Testing out things and ideas when the child's experience is limited and coping strategies are immature often results in annoying behavior that incurs the disapproval of parents. In addition, the child's feelings of anger, jealousy, and frustration find their outlet in negative behavior, also difficult for parents and children to cope with. Most parents are very familiar with responses such as "I don't want to" or "Why should I" or "I don't know" from children who are testing limits and/or parental authority.

Families generally have some form of structure and some rules of behavior. The purpose of rules or guidelines is to protect the child from her own impulsivity and inexperience so that she will not suffer irreparable damage physically, socially, and emotionally. Rule enforcement is one way parents can teach children impulse- and self-control, as well as increase their frustration tolerance. This training is extremely useful in the development of self-organization, concentration, and motivation.

The goals of discipline are to teach self-control, increase frustration tolerance; and to understand, and respect, the rights of others. Effective discipline requires consistency on the part of the parents. They must clearly delineate the difference between acceptable and unacceptable behavior. Behavior that is tolerated at one time and punished the next time results in confusion and eventual manipulation on the part of the child. Therefore, parents must clearly state and try to enforce only those rules that they believe in and are essential to the welfare of both the child and the family.

"Morals are caught, not taught" is one of those precepts that parents need to consider. The behavior being modeled by the parent is usually reflected by the child. Watching children play house dispels all doubt about the keenness with which children observe parental activities, attitudes, and principles. "Do as I say, but not as I do" is extremely confusing to your children. Breaking promises, making excuses, or using double standards results in inconsistency and encourages the child to test parental edicts. She is continually trying to find out what the parent really stands for and if she cannot get an honest answer, she is assailed by doubt and anxiety.

Good discipline corrects the child's behavior without undermining the child's integrity and self-esteem. We can label the behavior or the act as "foolish" or "stupid" without placing the child in the same category. Parents should help the child to understand that she is being corrected because the negative acts are destructive to her, and possibly to the entire family. Parents have a responsibility to protect the child from her own impulsivity and destructive feelings. By setting limits, and by guiding her impulses, parents can learn what the child's negative behavior is trying to express. Thus, the parent can help the child to find alternatives or use strategies that help her to overcome self-defeating actions.

When the child is acting out feelings of anger, frustration, disappointment, and rejection, she is really expressing her inability to deal with these feelings in a constructive way. It is useless for the parent to "punish" her because she expressed anger. It would be infinitely more helpful if parents let the child know they understand why she is angry, but at the same time help the child to channel that anger in ways that are least damaging to all concerned. This approach requires empathy, understanding, maturity, and self-control on the part of the parents, who need to model the behavior that they expect from their child.

When parents establish definite rules of behavior, it is important that they also make clear the consequences of breaking these rules. This will eliminate entanglements in arguments, which usually disintegrate into a battle of wills. Arguments between parent and child undermine parental authority and increase the child's anxiety. If the child wins she may become anxious because, psychologically, she has become her own parent (a responsibility for which she is not ready). If she loses, her self-esteem and sense of autonomy are undermined and the parent has set up communication barriers that erode the child's sense of trust. Thus, neither one wins—in fact both are losing. *If the child senses that the parents will back down, she is apt to create a super-spectacle that may result in extreme guilt feelings on the part of both the child and parents.* In many cases, this type of interaction causes passivity and extended dependence, and reduces the child's motivation to work productively in school. The child is not learning self-control, respect for authority, or using coping skills in solving her problems.

In the event that punishment is needed to correct the child, it should be in keeping with the offense. For example, it is out of proportion to prevent the child from going out after school for a month because she came home late from school. This will only confuse the child, especially if a lesser punishment is given for more serious misbehavior. In addition, punishment that needs to be enforced over a period of time is very difficult for both parent and child. In her angry state the child is bound to be disruptive and additional punishment makes the application of discipline unwieldy and unmanageable. Thus, the child learns to manipulate the adults who appear to be capricious and inconsistent, and the child's goal becomes "don't get caught."

This type of interaction is not conducive to encouragement, compliments, understanding, and nurturance between parent and child. The child learns that only negative behavior succeeds in getting parental attention rather than positive and cooperative behavior. Her self-confidence is undermined and social interaction becomes difficult. Children understand, respond, and respect parental honesty, fairness, and control. They respect, imitate, and feel secure with parents who are sincere and loving when they set limits, provide structure, and enforce discipline. Remember that "no" can be a "love" word!

Some Guidelines

1. Rules of behavior should be clear, reasonable, consistent, and enforceable.
2. The consequences of rule breaking also should be equally clear, fair, consistent, and enforceable.
3. Do not wait until you are out of patience and/or angry before you enforce the rule. Enforcement or administration of consequences should be done calmly, firmly, and lovingly.
4. Use self-control. Try to model the behavior you are expecting from the child. Screaming, yelling, or throwing things should be avoided.
5. Avoid physical punishment if at all possible.
6. Respect your child's integrity; avoid derogative labels.
7. Listen to what your child is saying and emphathize with her feelings.
8. Avoid making the child ashamed of her feelings. Accept and help her to understand them and to seek out less destructive, alternative ways of expressing them.
9. Help your child understand the motive for her behavior and how to deal with it. Be sure to set enforceable limits.
10. When you realize her "bad" behavior is calculated to attract attention, find more positive ways of giving her attention before she acts out. Do not carry a grudge.
11. Help her discuss and resolve her problems by teaching her problem-solving strategies.
12. Do not make promises you can't keep. If you have to break a promise, always be sure you discuss it with the child and respond to her feelings.

Helping Children to Deal
with Death and Loss

Death is a realistic and normal part of life. Preparing children to understand and cope with this inevitable trauma is essentially an ongoing task that parents need to understand and to accept. By age three most children are aware that people and other living objects die. They have seen flowers and plants fade away, birds or pets may have died, and loved relatives (such as a grandparent) may have passed on. These events often elicit puzzling questions that parents find difficult and often leave unanswered—or they answer in a vague and unsatisfactory manner. Avoiding or postponing the child's questions not only discomfort the parent, but create uncertainty and anxiety in the child.

Children's normal response to death and loss is extremely subjective and personal. "Where and why did they leave?" "What caused him to go?" "Was it my fault?" "Will I die, too?" "Will my mother/father die now?" "What will happen to me?" These are all questions that trigger fear, guilt, and anxiety in the child that he may not always verbalize. It is essential that parents have formulated some explanation that will quiet and reassure the child without being dishonest. Whether the response is within the religious, existential, or common framework, it may help parents if they can see death as a normal outcome of living, or as part of the normal life cycle that begins with birth and, as far as we can tell, culminates with death. When parents do this within the context of daily life events (such as the end of seasons, or the end of weeks and years), the child begins to formulate, with some understanding, that there is a beginning and ending that is normal for all life. He will understand that it is the nature of the universe, and accept death as inevitable and normal, something that has nothing to do with his being good or bad, helpful or not helpful. Parental attitudes often determine how the child will react. Normal grieving is an essential part of accepting a loss, and is necessary in order to start anew. However, hysterical, self-blaming, and guilt-ridden reactions tend to create intense fear and anxiety. Sharing pain and tears, and expressing how much the loved one will be missed, help children to express their own feelings of grief, and eventually permit them to restore themselves to the tasks of living.

Long before the death of a family member, opportunities may arise that could help a child to understand and deal with death. When a pet or stray animal dies he may wish to conduct a mock funeral. In order to find out what really happens to the dead pet, the child may wish to exhume it, and in this way learn the finality of death. The questions arising from such activity and their discussion can prepare parents to deal with the loss of a family member.

The grief reaction of children resembles that of adults and can be described in five stages. The first is denial and isolation. To avoid the pain of the loss or separation, the child denies the event with the idea that by isolating himself from the reality of the event, somehow it did not really happen, and that therefore it cannot be real or true.

At the second stage the child's sense of total helplessness envelops him in intense anger. I cannot make my parents see that I need to feel trusted and forgiven, and that they validate and understand my judgments. "How could he die and leave me alone?" Anger at being left may conceal feelings of guilt based on ordinary acts of defiance or thoughtlessness. He may feel that had he behaved better he could have prevented this, so he is angry with himself as well.

The third stage of grief reaction involves bargaining. The child may bargain away the reality of the death or loss by resolving and making promises of impeccable behavior in order to restore the life of his loved one. This effort is soon dispersed as the reality and finality of the situation sinks in, and the person does not return.

This initiates the fourth stage—depression (anger turned back on the self). Though the depression is an effort to handle the child's guilt, it does represent the sadness inherent in loss or a gradual understanding of the reality of the event requiring a reordering of his life. In most instances depression heralds the final stage of grief, which is the resolution—the acceptance and integration of the loss. Now the child can talk about "his father or mother," or whatever, and even review the events leading to the death.

These stages do not always appear in the order presented but they all do take place. It is important that the adults in the child's life do not ignore the child's grief or allow him to grieve in his own way. He may show unreasonable fears, or make unrealistic demands, for example, wanting the lights on all night; or sleeping in the deceased's bed; or wearing items belonging to the loved person; or even refusing to be alone in the house. These requests will be short-lived if understood, and allowing them will enable the child to express his grief and return to more normal activities.

Some children may appear to have accepted the death intellectually, but painful psychological feelings may persist, which he represses. The beginning of true resolution is evidenced by the child recalling and discussing pleasant memories of his loved one. An awareness of the emotional complexity of loss will enable parents to prepare their children to accept the phenomenon of death and help them to come to grips with what appears to be a natural and inevitable part of the life cycle.

Based on Explaining Death to Children, *edited by E. Grolman. Boston: Beacon Press, 1969.*

Meeting 5
Discipline and Problems
of Sexuality

A. Greetings and opening remarks.
   1. Leader continues format of checking attendance, and summarizing previous meeting and discussion handouts.
   2. Parents may continue to volunteer to role-play an incident with their child during the week.
B. Topical presentation: Discipline and problems of sexuality.
   1. Due to the nature of these topics parents will ask many questions.
   2. Leader will encourage the recounting of actual exchanges between parent and child throughout the discussion.
C. Discussion highlights.
   1. Parental example is a powerful model for children's behavior throughout their lives.
   2. Parental discipline should not destroy self-esteem. It is an act of loving concern.
   3. Parents should discipline the act without undermining the child's integrity.
   4. Discipline should improve the child's self-control and frustration tolerance.
   5. Parents should be sensitive to the child's feelings (both negative and positive) and not make child ashamed of his feelings.
   6. Focus should be on helping the child to seek constructive alternative solutions to problems, rather than saying "Do as I say."
   7. Parents should mean what they say and say exactly what they mean.
   8. Parents are advised *not* to postpone discipline until they are very angry; rather, they should follow through after the first warning is given.
   9. Consistency and fairness are respected and understood by children.
   10. Leader explains sexual development as a concomitant part of growth.
   11. Sexuality is present at birth.
   12. The child's exploration of body parts is normal.
   13. Anxiety, fear, or other traumas sometimes cause the child to seek comfort from body parts (for example, touching genitals, thumb sucking, and the like).
   14. Questions on emerging sexuality should be answered honestly and simply in terms of the child's age and developmental stage. (For example, "Where do babies come from?")
   15. Sexual attitudes and practices are modeled by parents.

D. Human relations training.
    1. Leader continues to use role-playing in discussing questions emerging from the group.
E. Preparation for next meeting.
    1. Distribute handouts.
    2. Assign parents to bring in actual experiences.
F. Suggested parent handouts for meeting 6.
    1. Initiative vs. Guilt
    2. The Father's Role
    3. When a Child Begins School
    4. Getting Along with Your Child's Teachers
    5. Be Their Mother, Not Their Servant!

TV's Influence on Children

There is little doubt that the censorship and control exercised by concerned parent groups over the excessive violence and abusive language portrayed on children's TV programs has gotten results. However, recent research indicates that the most effective control of TV's influence on children comes from *within* the home rather than from outside censorship. Teamwork between the home and the media has proven to be the most effective way for parents to control the programs watched by their children. Because every family's needs, values, and customs are different, and because TV programs are subject to rapid changes, it is neither possible nor realistic to expect that child-rearing parents or even government officials can determine which programs are good and which are bad for children.

Parents need to realize that the guidelines for "good" TV diet are similar to those of good nutrition. How much TV should children watch? What kinds of programs are appropriate? And should they have a TV in their own room?—These questions can be equated to such questions as Would you give a child his own refrigerator? Would you allow him to eat any type of food indiscriminately, in the amount he wishes? Obviously most parents would not agree to the latter choice because they are committed to providing children with good nutrition to insure their physical growth and development. Similarly, the analogy of ensuring a good TV diet for the children's social and intellectual growth is of equal value.

Research studies reveal that children model their TV viewing habits of their parents. Consequently, when parents are upset about their young child watching too much TV, it is important that they note how much TV they watch (this usually does not apply to teenagers because they are at the stage of rebelling against parental values). The following guidelines may be useful in helping parents decide which programs to choose and how much TV their children should watch.

Do You Use TV Viewing as a Reward, or Do You Restrict
TV Programs to Punish Bad Behavior?

Such practices are counter to psychological theory. Appropriate rewards or punishments should relate as closely as possible to the behavior of the child. For example, if the child deliberately breaks a valued object, an appropriate punishment would be to have him replace or pay for its replacement through his allowance or some service for which he could get paid. Denial of a TV program would not be relevant to such a misdemeanor; in fact, at times it may work against the very principles the parents would normally uphold. They may be denying him an outstanding TV program such as a documentary or a special event program assigned to him by his teacher. Thus, the parents may have to rescind their punishment or deny themselves, the child, and the rest of the family a worthwhile program.

Furthermore, this practice places too much emphasis and value on the medium. Parents who use TV as a reward may find that the programs for that particular evening are totally inappropriate for their young child. In this case the child may feel he cannot trust his parents to keep promises made to him for good behavior.

Do You Interrupt, Interpret, or Mediate the Programs Watched by Your Children?

The young child will gain far more understanding and knowledge when the parents or older siblings rephrase the dialogue, define difficult words, or explain the events they have viewed. This process of "direct mediation" is highly effective with young children because they are curious, learn rapidly, and have great confidence in the information and attitudes of significant adults such as parents and teachers. However, with teenagers "indirect mediation" is recommended. Again, at this age children are more resistant to adult statements and reject being "lectured." However, when adults comment on the programs to each other or another family member the teenager inadvertently overhears and internalizes the commentaries. TV programs will generally make more of an impact upon children when their parents share their comments and views.

Research indicates that preschool children have difficulty distinguishing the "real" events portrayed on TV programs from the "unreal" events, such as TV commercials. Children as old as seven or eight seem unable to perceive, organize, and understand the information on TV programs. Therefore, the adult can decidedly influence and affect the young child's attitudes by commenting on the programs.

Do You Give Consent by Remaining Silent?

Because our society endorses the right of each citizen to express his views, much of what is presented on TV does not necessarily reflect our views, beliefs, or value system. However, many parents react with silence when a TV presentation is in opposition to their sense of decorum. Overt, spontaneous parental reaction to such programs is much better than silence, which can mislead our children. Similarly, a pleasing program should be responded to with approval.

It is important for parents to familiarize themselves with the contents of the weekly TV guide to ensure purposeful viewing for their children. Thus, they can select the programs they will view as a family, as well as those programs that will entertain, interest, and inform their children.

Furthermore, parents should critique and voice their opinion of these programs and encourage their children to do the same. This can result in the family discussion of topics that otherwise might be overlooked or unappreciated. Such topics as drugs, teenage pregnancy, and safety precautions are common TV events that can be used as springboards for discussions and communication between parents and teenagers.

In conclusion, parents need to call the signals and guide their children in reference to how much TV and which TV programs their children watch at home. By voicing and sharing their reactions and criticisms they will help their children to become more discerning and discriminating between worthwhile and worthless, time-consuming programs. Such interaction can help make TV a source of wholesome recreation as well as informed enlightenment.

Rules for Keeping Poisons
and Children Apart

Every year thousands of young children exploring the mysteries of cupboards and cabinets around the house manage to get into more than simple mischief. A variety of harmful substances, ranging from corrosive acids to cosmetics and medicines are swallowed by these inquisitive youngsters. Poison Prevention Week, observed annually during the third week in March, serves to remind adults of their responsibilities for keeping poisons and children apart.

Most mothers who remember the stages their children went through may well vote for the "terrible two's" as one of the worst. One reason could be the penchant of these youngsters of around two for getting into medicine cabinets and onto the tops of dressers. More than 15,000 two-year-olds were treated for accidentally swallowing medicines, according to recent FDA figures. This was the largest number of cases in any product category and for any age group. Two-year-olds also accounted for the largest number of ingestions of cosmetics, although one-year-olds were not far behind.

These younger children, who are still at the crawling stage, are more likely to get into such things as cleaning and polishing agents, petroleum products, turpentine, and paint. These materials frequently are stored under bathroom or kitchen sinks, or in cupboards just at the eye level of an inquisitive child. It might come as a surprise that those lush green plants that have become increasingly popular as house decorations are another source of danger to young children. Ten percent of all reported ingestions in the under-five age group, 9,085 of them—involved plants. Five years previously only 4.5 percent of ingestions in that age group involved plants. Philodendron, yew, dieffenbachia, poinsettia, African violet, and begonia are among the plants that young children seem to like to nibble on.

In contrast, aspirin, which ranks as one of the most perilous causes of accidental poisoning among youngsters, has been less of a menace in recent years. Currently, it ranks fourth behind plants; soaps, detergents, and cleaners; and vitamins and minerals among those products most frequently consumed by youngsters. Deaths from aspirin among children under five also have dropped dramatically.

Progress obviously is being made in preventing accidental poisoning of young children, thanks to "child-proof" closures for medicine containers, educational efforts, and the vigilance of poison control centers throughout the nation. But the fact that tens of thousands of youngsters still get into hazardous substances around the home suggests that adults have a lot more to learn about protecting their children.

Educating the public, particularly parents, about how to prevent accidental poisoning is one of the tasks of the Division of Poison Control, which uses the mass media to provide educational messages to consumers and health professionals. The third week in March is devoted to the observance of Poison Prevention Week.

Today the activities associated with this special week are sponsored by the National Planning Council for Poison Prevention Week on which more than 20 concerned organizations, including the FDA, are represented. During the week the council distributes a wide variety of educational materials, including posters and leaflets, and provides material for use in the press.

The message these materials convey is one that all parents and other adults should pay heed to all year 'round:

- Keep potentially poisonous substances locked up. If your medicine or cleaning cabinets will not lock, find a place that does for storing these products.
- Keep hazardous substances in their original containers; never transfer them to a cup or beverage bottle or anything that might suggest to a child that the contents are something he can eat or drink.
- Keep internal medicines, such as over-the-counter painkillers or cough remedies, apart from other household products. Many of the containers look alike.
- Ask your pharmacist to provide safety caps on medicine containers.
- Dispose of unused medicines and household products by emptying the residue down the toilet or drain. Rinse the container before discarding it.
- Get rid of prescription medicines as soon as the illness for which they were prescribed is over. Not only does this remove a potential hazard for children, but over a period of time chemical changes can take place in the medicine which render it useless or even dangerous.
- Never tell a child medicine is candy or tastes like candy.
- As far as possible, keep house plants out of reach of small children.
- Teach youngsters early not to eat or drink anything that has not been given to them by a responsible person.
- Keep a one-ounce bottle of syrup of ipecac handy, but do not use it unless directed to do so by a poison control center or a physician.
- Keep the phone number of your local poison control center near the telephone in the event of an emergency.

Remember, the only way to prevent accidental poisonings from substances found about the house is to prevent children from getting into them. Or, to put it another way, for every child accidentally poisoned, there is an adult responsible.

By Annabel Hecht. H.E.W. Publication No. (FDA) 79–7023, U.S. Department of Health, Education, and Welfare.

Responding to Children's Sexuality

The embarrassment with which most parents approach the process of providing sex information to their children generally invests this subject with confusing double-bind messages, particularly for pubescent children. What seems to come across is that the physical expression of affection is not "safe" or "nice" to talk about. Paradoxically, though sexual customs and behaviors have encountered drastic changes in our generation, and though in practice, many taboos and restrictions have been relaxed, the open discussion of sex is still subject to a double standard. It seems OK and permissible to titillate but not OK to teach the honest facts. Suggestive advertisements in magazines, newspapers, and on TV, and in the movies that openly present recreational sex, or advertisements of contraceptive devices, all seem to imply it is more acceptable to have sex than to talk about it. Considering the importance of sexual behavior to life itself, sex education per se has been a touchy issue for schools and summarily managed by most parents.

It appears that knowledge of sex and its consequences and implications has been at a really elementary level. Despite the burst of information around us, venereal disease is more rampant among teenagers than among people of any other age. In a recent survey of those teenagers seeking clinical help, 37 percent did not know that women are more likely to conceive at ovulation, which occurs halfway through the menstrual cycle; 24 percent were not aware they could conceive the first time they had intercourse, and 24 percent had no knowledge that VD was transmitted through genital contact.

Teenagers bear one out of five U.S. babies. They have one out of three abortions. Infant mortality is higher among teenagers than babies born to mothers over twenty; maternal death due to complications is 60 percent higher than it is with mothers over twenty; and pregnant teenagers commit suicide seven times more than other teenagers.

Most teenagers who get pregnant while in high school are more likely to not complete their course or graduate; usually they go on welfare, and very few go to work. Less than one-half of them marry the fathers of their babies, and more than half of those who do are divorced within six years. Even though today many teenagers are sexually active, the ready availability of information per se is not helping them handle sexual issues in a mature way.

All pubescent children are curious and want to know the facts of life. In the past, few adults were either ready or willing to discuss sex openly and honestly. This made young people simultaneously angry and curious, even though still fearful of the power that sex had to warp and ruin their lives if they played around with it. The idea that the subject can be discussed publicly and privately, that people need to understand their own sexuality, and that they can reflect and have choices about it is revolutionary. The knowledge revolution has helped both parents and children. Books like *Our Bodies, Ourselves* have made it possible for us to connect feelings and values about reproduction and gender to related physical body functions. Public and private discussions of this private behavior help young people to understand their own sexuality. The responsibilities involved in their choices depend upon values, and values depend upon parental attitudes and openness.

Because the abundance of ready information on sex today has also added to the child's confusion, some schools have developed courses for both parents and children. The course for parents is intended to help them teach their children about sex in the context of health education. Health is defined as what one needs to know to stay healthy. It covers things that can endanger health (peer pressure, feelings, fear, embarrassment, choices of gratification) as well as sources of help. These programs are generally conducted by registered nurses for at least four hours. Following the course for parents, a nine-hour course of instruction is offered to their children. Such courses are designed to make it easier for parents to teach their own values about sex and its place in the total life cycle. Children really want to know what their parents believe and the idea that they can discuss this subject with those they trust the most enables them to deal with fallacies and peer pressure much more comfortably.

Schools, however, cannot and should not teach values, but only the physical and emotional facts about sex. It is the parents who must help the child to feel comfortable, to ask questions, and to enable them to get rid of the feeling that sex is dirty. They can help the child to discuss facts about masturbation, wet dreams, chemical body changes, and the difference beween lust and love. It is the parent's *responsibility to place sex within the context of mature love, respect, and affection, and to impress upon the child the responsibilities involved,* as well as its joys and positive aspects. School programs provide only the physical background, thus making the task of sex instruction easier for the parent.

Some compelling reasons why parents should be the most important source of sex values and information to their children are:

1. They have the opportunity to instruct them from early childhood on, and to answer questions however and whenever they arise.
2. They are in a position to be aware of the child's growth and needs and to meet these needs in terms that the child can understand.
3. They can give instruction and information in the context of their own philosophical, moral, and religious orientation at a time when the child is most open and responsive, and before she is influenced by the vast amount of conflicting information and ideas in today's society: By meeting the child's needs as they emerge, parents can make the topic a fact of life, rather than one of fear, shame, and self-doubt.

Some Reasons for Poor
Eating Habits

Some of the more common messages articulated by poor eating habits might be:

- I am jealous of a new baby—I wish I could be fed that way.
- I am very afraid of something I don't understand—everything scares me.
- I don't have any control over myself. They're leaning on me.
- Hey, this is fun. I've got them jumping through my hoop.
- I'm angry at everyone but don't know how to tell them.
- Maybe if they watch me, they'll stop that stupid fighting.
- I want everything to stay the way it is; I'm afraid of change.
- Help me control myself.
- Love me more openly.
- Hey there, look at me. I'm me. I'm a person. Can't you see that?

Your child and every other picky eater is trying to tell us something. So stop making any reference to the symptoms of his problem and try hard to respond to the real message.

His tastebuds are as healthy as yours or mine. His emotions are blunting his appetite. It is that simple, yet enormously complicated, which is why parents should not ignore the cause and try only to modify the symptoms.

CHARACTERISTICS OF YOUNG
SCHOOL-AGE CHILDREN

Experimental Learning about One's Body

Children at this age can differentiate body parts, and know their proper names and functions. Sex activities most often include autoerotic activity, mutual masturbation, and exhibitionism, and among boys, comparison in penis size and force of urinary stream.

Parents who exhibit themselves, talk excessively about sex, or are preoccupied with sex instruction tend to overstimulate their children.

Play

Play is better organized, and is imaginative and ingenious. Children now show high regard for rules and fair play. Leadership qualities are displayed. Their imagination is very active, especially their power of make-believe. They tend to favor physical play with peers; and they enjoy puzzles, intellectual games, and solitary activities.

Play has a variable meaning; it is not the same at all ages: the play of a two-year-old is quite different from that of a five-year-old. The play of small children often appears to be supportive of their thought processes. As the child's verbal ability increases with advancing age, her play takes increasingly organized forms, and she begins to take play roles. Anyone who has observed small children knows how complex this role-taking can become, with fairly complicated social situations being reproduced. The roles of play are sometimes executed in detail and with extravagant imagination. For example, the little girl having a tea party with her animals and dolls lays her tiny table with her doll dishes and puts a doll or a stuffed animal at each place, and then, acting the role of gracious hostess, picks up her teapot full of water and solicitously asks the teddy bear if he would have some tea. Then, putting down the teapot, she shifts her stance and walks around the table to stand behind the teddy bear, answering the questions she has just asked in a high, squeaky voice, and replying that indeed she (the teddy bear) would like some. This shift of speaking voice is projected to each doll or animal in the play, and serves to make the limits of the roles more distinct. In this way children learn how it feels to be in another person's place—and their understanding of social interaction begins to grow and expand, as they internalize adult values and attitudes that they unconsciously reenact when they become adults.

Interpersonal Relationships

The child begins to question parental admirations and begins to experience conflict of loyalty. Moral values are generalized as they are learned. The child views moral laws as absolute values in real things and existing as an indivisible part of the object. "Do not touch the plug"—the plug is something not to be touched.

Parents are equated more with peers and other adults, but continue to hold positions of importance. Adults are used as models of behavior, and the child is still dependent on them.

Obedience to Rules

Parents, and obedience to parents, are viewed as one. Disobedience is an infringement of adult authority rather than a violation of a moral obligation. Naughty words are a violation of adult-imposed taboos. Reproof and punishment are expected as natural consequences of misbehavior. The child's guilt makes her seek atonement; the child will indulge in self-punishment and/or obsessive-compulsive behavior. Through rituals she develops her own taboos about thoughts and acts, and endows them with compulsion, for example, not permitting herself objects or persons, or even to look at them. They impute magic power to thoughts and feelings (for example, the childish game of "don't step on a crack lest you break your mother's back!"). Such games have the element of self-punishment and magical protection. Piaget postulates a theory of the child's employment of imminent justice whereby she feels guilty and, subsequently, inflicts self-punishment.

Children generally conform to adult rules because of respect and constraint toward authority. However, they are confused by rules that adults have for themselves that seem elastic and not absolute. This can lead to their cheating and stealing because they have witnessed such acts by their parents. Parents are surprised and angry to see themselves played back as dishonest, unfair, and unfaithful.

Stealing

Stealing can represent defiance of authority, or the inability of a child to distinguish between what is hers, and what belongs to others. It may be that the child's place in the family is so undifferentiated from others that she does not distinguish herself as separate. She takes things as if they were hers because she sees them as belonging to the whole family. She feels she is borrowing them. However, this behavior can be an expression of needing more love and attention from parents.

Conscience

Conscience or the super-ego finds its anchor in the internalized rules and precepts that parents impose upon their children. A sense of morality is internalized as the child incorporates the values, standards, and expectations of her parents. Lack of such guidance interferes with the child's moral and ethical development. However, when parents are too repressive they tend to increase a child's sense of guilt and decrease her self-esteem. This can interfere with social development and learning.

Other Concerns

Parents find questions related to birth, sex, and death very difficult to explain to their children. Where did I come from? Will you die? Why do people die? What happens afterward? are questions that parents need to answer as honestly as possible within the context of their own philosophy. Children grieve the death of parents, relatives, and pets. Because they are still egocentric, children feel loss and sorrow often accompanied by guilt. They tend to accuse themselves to some degree for the loss of loved ones. Prolonged grief constitutes mental depression, and periods of discouragement and depression are not rare. There has been a marked rise in frequency of childhood and adolescent suicide. The child who has a well-developed sense of trust of competency and autonomy is the one who adapts to the realities of life best. She can accept the guidance, instruction, and affection of substitute adults.

Emergence of Cognition

Thinking and reasoning are coming together and are being acted out. The child coordinates her subjective version of the real world around her. Increasingly she acts in a consistent pattern of reasoning and behaves as if she intuitively knew what life was about. This marks the real beginning of cognition. The child often uses words and thoughts as substitutes for action!

Children think only of one idea at a time. Their perceptions are influenced by preconceptions, and their thinking is still egocentric and often at variance with that of adults.

Meeting 6
Initiative vs. Guilt

A. Greetings and opening remarks.
   1. Participants check off attendance.
   2. Leader summarizes principal points to date of four developmental stages and related issues covered.
   3. Reports of ongoing progress are encouraged around these issues.
   4. Leader introduces fifth developmental stage.
B. Topical presentation: Initiative vs. guilt.
C. Discussion highlights.
   1. Important parental role is to provide ample security so the child will feel safe with new or changing circumstances.
   2. Parents should praise generously but honestly.
   3. Parents encourage risk taking within normal limits.
   4. Parents should not minimize danger, but they need to help child to deal with it.
   5. Avoid being too overprotective.
   6. In order to learn, a child needs parental example and encouragement, but he must be allowed his own experience within limits set by parents.
   7. Father becomes more actively involved, assumes coleader role in the family.
   8. Parents should not shame the child when he fails, but should encourage him to analyze where he went wrong and encourage him to try again.
   9. Encourage initiative as a healthy concomitant of creativity so that child feels free to learn from his efforts and to keep on trying.
D. Human relations training.
   1. Parents are now eager to role-play.
   2. Parents report behaviors or specific illustrations of interactions with their children.
   3. Leader models empathic understanding and reflection of feelings.
   4. Leader helps parent to focus on meaning of behavior and to explore available alternatives.
   5. Parents become actively involved in searching for alternative modes of handling or responding to situations presented.
E. Preparation for next meeting.
   1. Distribute handouts.

F. Suggested parent handouts for meeting 7.
    1. Industry vs. Inferiority
    2. Raising Children
    3. The Angry Child
    4. Feelings of Guilt
    5. Stress

Background for topical presentation: The child is now beyond kindergarten and progressing to grade one. During this period, discovery of the environment and its limits intensifies. He begins to see what he can do for himself and for others; what he should do, and what he can get. His goals extend beyond the family, and socialization is becoming important. Play helps him to understand the world around him and to become aware of rules. He learns to use his *initiative* profitably and safely to meet his needs. Parental "dos and don'ts" are being organized into a system of principles that will serve to guide his personal and social behavior for the rest of his life. Conscience or the super-ego is becoming internalized and though he may feel resentful and angry when parents set limits, he is inwardly grateful.

Socially the child is differentiating relationships and ideas. He is learning to compete and as his sense of confidence improves, his guilt (or feelings of inadequacy) decrease. Parents should be careful not to constantly fault, shame, or ridicule his efforts. This results in growing feelings of inadequacy, which increase his sense of guilt. Negative personality characteristics such as unwillingness to take a chance, to try new things, to risk failure, to be creative, or to participate in new activities can result. If the child's sense of conscience is developed to the extreme, his judgment may be impaired and he will be excessively cautious—or foolhardy!

INITIATIVE VS. GUILT

Stage four is known as the genital stage in classical psychoanalysis. The child of age four to five is pretty much master of her body. She usually can ride a tricycle, run, cut, and hit. Thus, she can initiate motor activities of various sorts on her own and no longer merely responds to, or imitates, the actions of other children. The same holds true for her language and fantasy activities. According to Erikson, the emerging social dimension at this stage is initiative as opposed to guilt. The child now is realizing that she can initiate action of various kinds on her own, and depending on the outcome of this action, can receive approbation or reproof. In other words, her reaction can make her feel good or guilty.

Whether the child emerges from this stage with her sense of initiative far outbalancing her sense of guilt depends to a considerable extent upon how parents respond to her new self-initiated activities. Children who are given much freedom and opportunity to initiate motor play such as running, bike riding, sliding, skating, tussling, and wrestling have their sense of initiative reinforced. Initiative is also reinforced when parents answer their children's questions (intellectual initiative) and do not deride or inhibit fantasy or play activity. On the other hand, if the child is made to feel that her physical activity is bad, that her questions are a nuisance, and that her play is silly and stupid, then she may develop a sense of guilt over self-initiated activities. In general, this feeling will persist through later life stages. This tends to make the child fearful of experimentation or risk taking; she tends to reject or fear new situations and ideas because she is afraid to venture beyond what she feels will be approved. Consequently she tends to be rigid and unimaginative.

THE FATHER'S ROLE

Throughout the last thirty years the family as an institution has undergone many drastic changes. Developments in the scientific, social, economic, and educational areas have exerted their impact. Prior to this, parental roles were fairly well defined. The mother was considered to be the children's primary source of affection, nurturance, and physical care. The father was the family's breadwinner, protector, decision maker, and representative in the outer world.

Studies on early childhood factors that affect psychological and cognitive growth have centered largely on the mother's role. However, the many unanswered questions regarding the influence of the father upon the personality development of the child have led to a renewed examination of his position and influence in the life of the modern family. Other factors include the diminishing size of the family itself, which discourages the father's authoritarian role; the increasing number of working mothers, which results in fathers becoming more involved in household activities; the new emphasis on a democratic family structure; the tremendous increase in the rate of divorce and separation with as many fathers being awarded custody of the children as mothers; and the nature of the modern marriage relationship itself, which has increased the risks and hazards of an institution formerly considered fairly impervious to change.

John V. Gilmore, in a 1980 publication of the Gilmore Institute (*The Father's Role in the Family*), writes: "A survey of the large body of research literature dealing with the father's current role in the family makes possible some generalizations—among the most important of which are the following:

1. "The father now plays a far more intimate and nurturant, caretaking type of role in the family than did his own father or any of his forebears.

2. "His relationship with his children is inextricably dependent on the stability and success of his own marriage.

3. "His attitude toward and communication with each individual child constitute a separate subsystem within the family system as a whole.

4. "The dichotomy of parental roles in the traditional family structure in which father was breadwinner and mother the nurturant, home-based parent is sharply modified and no longer exists.

5. "All studies indicate the importance of the father's close relationship with each child in a caretaking role from the time of birth.

6. "The father's influence is vital in the formation of his children's gender identity. His nurturance and warmth toward daughter and/or son are more important influences than his own emotional security.

7. "The effects on children of prolonged father absence—either physical or psychological—are damaging and more or less permanent. Identity, social responsibility, and cognitive style are all adversely affected, especially if the absence occurs at a young age for the child.

8. "The distant, detached, uncaring father, together with a son's inappropriate involvement with a "close-binding-intimate" mother are known to be a cause of homosexuality in boys. The reverse situation is a factor in lesbianism among girls.

9. "Paternal warmth is known to be associated with generosity and high moral standards among children.

10. "Extreme dominance and control by either parent stifle children's initiative, intellectual development, problem-solving skills, and social responsibility."

WHEN A CHILD BEGINS SCHOOL

This September more than six million five- and six-year-olds will make their first significant venture into foreign territory: they will leave home to begin kindergarten or first grade. That a large percentage of them adjust to school with minimum difficulty is a tribute to the resiliency of the young child. Unfortunately, parents (who play a major role in this drama) seldom receive the support they need to help both themselves and their children to effectively handle this new experience.

When the child leaves home comfortably and is eager for the new experiences school will bring, everything is lovely. But when the child becomes anxious and fearful or refuses to go to school—or if he or she goes amid such emotional scenes that both the child and parent are physically and emotionally drained—something has gone astray. Unless the situation receives immediate attention, a temporary crisis may become a chronic problem. (This may lead to what is usually called "school avoidance" or "school phobia"—terms that simply mean that for one reason or another, the child is anxious about the separation from home and is afraid to go to school.)

What can parents do to help their child take this developmental step forward? First, parents should understand that there are certain tasks that must be mastered at certain ages. No matter what our ages, each of us has a job to do—a task or tasks to master. Each period of life brings its own challenges and stresses—from infancy, when the baby must learn to trust her world and the helping people in it, to young adulthood, when the young person must decide on career goals and life styles. The building blocks for sound personality development involve the successful mastery of these tasks at each level of growth and development.

Thus, the five- or six-year-old has a major job: to go to school. In order to do this task as society has set for him or her, the child must successfully master three earlier tasks. First, he or she must make the shift from dependency upon parents and the home to dependency upon peers and other adults. This means that the school-age child must allow other people to meet many of her needs and to relate to her in meaningful fashion. How easily this task is mastered depends in large measure upon how secure and trusting her early relationships have been, and how unambivalent her parents are about supporting her new venture.

The second task for the child entering school is the management of separation anxiety. For most children this is accomplished with a mininum of anxiety or distress. For others, however, the threat of the loss of mother is terribly frightening and extremely stressful, both for the child and for the mother. Separation anxiety is one of the most painful experiences a child can have. Often parents, who can see no logical reason for it, find it is a most baffling experience.

Finally, the school-age child must learn to accept the authority of other adults, namely, the teacher, principal, and other support personnel in the school. This acceptance is made easier if the child has had a healthy dose of basic trust through her early relationships with other helping adults.

These, then, are the young child's jobs. But parents have their job, too, and that is to do everything they can to make it possible for the child to deal effectively with his or her new experiences. How can parents do this? In response to questions from many parents, I began some years ago, in late spring, to meet with parents of preschoolers to discuss how they could help prepare their children for entry into school. Here are some practical suggestions—some "*dos*" and "*don'ts*"—that we discussed and that have proven effective for many parents.

- Do not make the beginning of school a topic of daily conversation during the summer months. Do not belabor the issue—or, as one child said to his overzealous mother, "Don't make a federal case out of it!"

- Do treat going to school as part of the normal course of events, something that is expected and something that parents casually accept that the child will be doing (with some support and encouragement).

- Do not allow older children to frighten or tease the younger child with tales of how awful school is. If necessary, speak with the older children privately about their responsibility in helping the younger child go to school without fear. Try to make the older children your allies. If a teasing child is a neighborhood bully over whom you have no control, invite your child to trust your perceptions about what school will be like, rather than accepting what the other child has to say on the subject.

- Do answer honestly all questions the child asks about school and what to expect. Knowing the number of days she will attend, the length of time she will be away from home, how she will get back and forth to school—all are important, for a child may be made anxious by uncertainty and needs to know details in order to master her anxiety. Many schools hold orientation sessions for parents and children to acquaint them with school staff members, the classroom the child will be attending, and school procedures.

  Working mothers and fathers will also want to make certain that the child knows the arrangement for before- and/or after-school care.

- Do not give the impression that there is any choice about whether or not to attend school. Children will often say, "I'm not going," or "They can't make me." These comments should be responded to calmly and reassuringly, letting the child know that you understand her concerns about this new situation but that you know she will be able to handle it—and that all children have to go to school. You may want to add that there is a law (or rule) that requires that children attend school. At five and six, children are already learning to respect and appreciate laws and rules. The point is not to waiver; wise parents do not offer a choice that they cannot or will not honor. The parent who wants a child to eat eggs does not say, "Would you like an egg for breakfast?" Instead, she or he asks casually, "How would you like your egg this morning: fried, scrambled, or boiled?" Do not argue the issue of school attendance. A calm, matter-of-fact, positive attitude is your goal.

● Do make transportation plans clear to the child. If he or she is to walk to school, walk the route together once or twice before school begins, or walk her to school and meet her there after classes have ended the first day or so. If there are other children from your neighborhood who are her age and who are walking, see if your child and a friend could walk together.

Do not set a pattern of walking into the classroom and standing around while the child gets seated. This may lead to tears or clingy behavior, which gets the child off on the wrong foot with other children, who then may tease her, thus adding to the problem. Goodbyes are best said at home or in the schoolyard.

If a child is transported to school by bus, help the child identify the type of vehicle and, if possible, take a bus ride with the child prior to the first day of school to alleviate some anxiety. If there are other children whom you know waiting for the bus, introduce your child to them. Older children may be encouraged to watch over younger ones. Once the bus arrives, be direct; say goodbye and allow the child to board by herself. If the child does cry, be assured that in most cases the tears will usually disappear before the bus is out of sight.

● Do not try to force the child to be exuberant about going to school. It is natural for a child not to be ecstatic about giving up a comfortable and safe relationship at home for the uncertain territory of school. Allow, even encourage, her to express all her feelings about school. One good way of allowing children to let off steam is through fantasy—and you need not be afraid of granting in fantasy that which you cannot grant in reality. In other words, acknowledge a child's right to wish for things or to wish that things were different, even when you cannot allow the wish to be fulfilled. For example, when the uptight six-year-old says, the day before school begins, "I wish nobody ever invented school or teachers," the wise parent will understand the underlying concern in such a statement and respond, perhaps in the following fashion:

"I wish nobody ever invented schools or teachers," says the child.

"It would be fun, wouldn't it, if we could just stay home and play all day and have nobody telling us what to do. Some days I feel that way, too. But we can't do all the things we'd like to, even though it's fun to think about the idea."

Sometimes just being able to say whatever is on his or her mind and to discover that the words are heard and the feelings are accepted is both calming and reassuring to a child.

● Many parents who work at home look forward to the free time they will have once their child enters school. However, do not tell the child how much fun you are going to be having while he or she is in school. Do let the child know that while she is doing her job at school, you will be doing yours. Mention of concrete tasks can be very reassuring to the child: "While you're in school today, I'll do the laundry and vacuuming so we can have some time together when you get home."

Parents who work outside the home often make special arrangements that allow them to be home the first day or two when their child returns from school. When this is not possible, other ways of giving a little extra attention can be found, such as a telephone call from work to the child who has just completed her first day at school, or an arrangement to do something special with the child later in the day when the parents return home from work.

Do create a normal routine atmosphere at home the first few days of school. This does not mean that you deny or avoid the uniqueness of the first day of school but, on the other hand, do not give the child the impression that her leaving for her first day of school is of the same magnitude as Lindbergh's solo flight across the Atlantic. One such family of a five-year-old arrived en masse at the school for the child's first day, formed a line on the sidewalk and waved and cried as their movie camera recorded his slow disappearance into the school! The parents' responsibility is to provide reassuring support when needed, but otherwise to "play it cool."

● Do not assume that all of the anxiety associated with a child's entry into school is the child's. Parents—especially mothers—may experience some anxiety of their own over their child's moving into a new era. This is understandable for the mother has to give up some of her control of the child to school authorities and to share her child's teaching and upbringing with others. Often she also has major read-justments to make in her own life if she now has a large portion of her time free.

Mothers need to separate their own anxiety from that of the child's. A mother's worry and tension are highly contagious and the young child quickly perceives and responds to them. I encourage mothers to acknowledge and accept their own feelings and reactions, get the youngster off to school—and then to relax and share their feelings with a friend.

What I am suggesting here is that a child's going off to school represents a developmental phase for parents as well as children. Parents should be aware that sending a child off to school can be anxiety provoking for them. Each parent maintains many childhood memories, both positive and negative, about school. A child's entry into school seems to reactivate for some parents the feelings they had when they started school themselves, particularly feelings associated with negative experiences—which, perhaps, leave the deepest impression. Therefore, in remembering their school experiences parents may have ambivalent feelings concerning their child's new experience. Because the parents' reaction to the child's early school experience is of critical importance to his or her early school adjustment, parents might profit by reviewing their own anxieties and satisfactions regarding their school entry experiences.

By the time their first child begins school, most parents have been away from the educational system for a number of years. When their child enters kindergarten or first grade, parents see a school that has probably changed considerably from what they remember. It would be helpful if parents could see this as a positive opportunity to re-acquaint themselves with the educational system and to get to know the school staff members and other parents involved in their child's school.

Though the focus here has been on the child entering kindergarten or first grade, we must realize that, for increasing numbers of children, kindergarten does not represent their first school experience. Today many children attend nursery schools, day-care centers, and other preschool programs. A happy preschool experience may promote a comfortable transition into kindergarten; however, kindergarten is not a repeat of nursery school.

As one very bright second-grader explained when asked about the differences between nursery school and kindergarten, "Well, most anybody can make it in nursery school. But when you go to real school, you're not so sure you can learn everything and make good grades."

Parents whose children have adjusted well to preschool are often surprised that the children may experience separation anxiety when they approach kindergarten or first grade. This repetition of emotional experience is an important developmental phenomenon. These children have endured the initial separation from home to receive the gratification of new experiences and friends, and they have dealt with their first major loss of persons outside their home. Children who have attended preschool and are entering kindergarten are in effect being asked to risk separation again for new horizons that have not been defined.

If parents do enroll a child in a preschool program, they should, if possible, select one that is as compatible as possible with the school their child will later attend. If the parents themselves are aware of whatever major differences exist, they can forewarn the child and, thus, help her to cope with them. The intention of preschool programs should be to provide a bridge between home and the world, one that might help children toward a kindergarten adjustment without infringing on local kindergarten experiences.

What happens if, after all this good planning and careful handling, the big day arrives and the child begins to cry or to complain of being sick? Parents should grit their teeth, fight back the annoyance, and PUSH. This means that the child is to go even if tears flow. Usually the "moment of truth" occurs at the point of separation between mother and child. Once this separation is made, the child usually recovers quickly and has a successful day. Many a mother or father who feels terrible all day because the child left in tears would be reassured if they could know that the tears have usually subsided before the child had gone two blocks away, and that the teacher was unaware that the child had experienced difficulty in getting to school that day. In a situation such as this, the first few days are critical. With firm, patient, reassuring handling of the child by parents and teachers, this fearful, tearful behavior usually disappears within a few days. By then the child has learned to feel comfortable away from home, she has learned to trust her teacher, and has made some new friends—and she has learned that some interesting, exciting things go on in her classroom. What is important for the child's emotional health is to feel good inside about herself and secure in her world with the support he or she has mastered.

In rare instances when this smooth process does not occur, when the anxiety does not abate after a few days, and the child's fearfulness and feelings of distress continue to mount, the problem child may be developing a more serious problem. At this point, parents should seek professional advice by asking for a consultation with the school guidance counselor, if the school has such a person, or other school personnel. A consultation with the family doctor or pediatrician might also be considered. However, for most children who have experienced basically stable and supportive relationships prior to entering school, and whose parents have dealt successfully with their own ambivalent feelings about the child's entry into school, their upset—if obvious at all—usually disappears quickly, particularly if the techniques described here are used consistently by parents and other supportive persons.

By Luleen Anderson, Ph.D.

GETTING ALONG WITH
YOUR CHILD'S TEACHERS

Many parents find it hard to involve themselves with their child's school because they seem complex and bureaucratic and are often housed in imposing buildings. They are generally regarded as much more substantial and powerful than individuals could ever be. Like bureaucracies, schools tend to give undue attention to routines and standard procedures and tend to resist change. Nevertheless, this does not mean that schools cannot change or that parents cannot be effective advocates of change through constructive input. Home–school relationships can and should be productive partnerships—if parents take the time and effort to make them work.

Generally speaking, cooperative social relationships are based on equity and a balance of power, and institutions respect power. So parents should begin to strengthen their relationship with their child's school by acknowledging and exerting a sense of shared ownership. When this is done with style, without irritability and with a feeling of confidence in their right to be there, they can communicate their ideas and expectations and be treated as full partners. Parents should know their child's school, and make sure to let the school know them!

Parent anonymity will not do a thing for either you or your child. So, keep the following points in mind.

1. Get to know your child's teacher through visits.

2. Show up and make connections with your child's school and let her know you consider school activities important. Games, concerts, fairs, returning late books and lost baseball bats, or the willingness to board class pets over vacation all offer means of making connections.

3. Show you really care! Keep up with school developments by letting school personnel know you. They will welcome your interest! When you meet your child's teacher, make specific references to what he or she is teaching and how your child is responding.

4. Attend meetings and familiarize yourself with the issues, and share your views on the issues.

5. Read and follow through on all school notices. Encourage your child to bring information home by paying prompt attention to it.

6. Know the principal and administrative staff. He or she often sets the tone for the whole school. Show your interest and desire to help.

7. Show your appreciation of the good things that happen. Teachers seldom get positive letters of appreciation. Be known as a supporter of the school. It is a great plus when you want to resolve a problem.

8. Join the PTA, and actively promote their efforts to act on behalf of your children's (and their teachers') needs. In certain schools, federal and state legislation require parent advisory councils and give them defined responsibilities.

Home–School relations should be a joint responsibility of the parents. Neither the father or mother should be reluctant to ask their employers for time off to attend to school business. Your joint participation contributes to your children's success. More employers are realizing that smoother school progress for the children generally results in less preoccupied employees. Furthermore, children who do well in school tend to have fewer absences.

Parent–Teacher Conferences

Conferences are the heart of parent–school relations, and generally, are of three types: those initiated by the teacher because of some problem; the periodic meeting, often scheduled at the close of marking periods; and the parent-initiated meeting, prompted by questions you have about your child's progress.

●   The conference will be more successful if you: review your child's homework and tests, noting any areas of concern. If there is incomplete work, raise the question of overplacement. Are there skill gaps? If items copied from the chalkboard into his notebook are garbled, consider an eye examination.

●   Talk with you child about his current concerns such as "What do you like most and least?" "What is hardest for you?" "Tell me about your friends." Questions of this type give you information about what to explore at the conference.

●   Have a notebook labeled "School Questions" that contains good and bad news, things you wonder about, or puzzles about the program. On conference day your notes can provide clarity and focus. Similarly, have samples of your child's work to review.

●   Both you and the teacher are experts on your child, each from different perspectives. Conferences should not be contests between parent and teacher. Teachers see the child in relation to his contemporaries. You see him as you hope he is! Do your part to set things at ease, and start with some positive feedback for the teacher.

●   Discouraging information is hard to take and becomes a crucial factor in many parent–teacher conferences. Teachers know parents get upset and are threatened by their child's poor school progress, and they may play down bad news. Candor is required between home and school, as the acknowledgment that children's learning is not the isolated responsibility of the child or a matter of blame. It is a matter of mutual concern for child, parent, and teacher.

- Plan specific follow-up. When things are not going well, concrete support is needed, not vague theories. When there is no improvement, seek a second opinion. If you and the teacher are not satisfied with your child's progress, you both should seek further help from specialists, such as a counselor or a psychologist.

- Teacher–parent conferences usually do not include the elementary school child. However, when the child is age fourteen or older, most schools allow him the option of attending such meetings.

- Critical incidents, such as accusations, unexpected warning notices, or accidents all require prompt attention. When such incidents occur, you need to support your child emotionally and find out the details at the conference. Telephones are fine for informational purposes but in academic, emotional, or disciplinary matters, face-to-face meetings are essential.

School Records Are Important

Although local procedures vary, schools have responded well to the 1974 Family Education Rights and Privacy Act allowing parents access to their children's school records. When any misunderstandings occur, parents should know they have the right to review their child's school file, especially when the child is transferred to a new school where his records may influence his placement.

Political Action Is Part of Home–School Relations, Too

Other ways parents can help:

- Watch those school budgets. In their effort to cut costs, officials make many decisions based on financial reasons rather than on what students need. Find out from the superintendent, the school committee, or the teacher how those proposed cuts will affect your child's education!

- Parental attendance at schoolboard meetings is important. You should follow board decisions closely, watch issues, study the public minutes, and examine the agenda. Share your views. Alert other parents to upcoming matters.

- Get school facts from more than one source, including teachers. It is not uncommon to find that teachers and administrators do not always have the same priorities.

- Letters in support of the schools to local papers usually help to secure needed improvements. Give deserving teachers public praise. They are crucial partners in your child's education. School politics can abound with double talk. Parents need to keep alert to the real issues.

Above All, School Must Be
the Domain of Our Children

Parent activism is basic to sound home–school relations, but the focus of this relationship should be the development of the child. It is important to remember that all children are different. Each child has his individual timetable and his own style of learning. One universal rule is that children function best when they are respected and supported, not forced. Yet, it is very difficult for parents not to compare their child with his group, particularly when he is not doing well. "Is the school doing its job? Who is at fault? Why is the child failing? Parents need to become more objective and try to understand the inherent rhythm and style of their child's individual learning pattern and allow him to progress at his own pace.

A good school centers on the child. The parents' task is to seek a working relationship, rather than be at war with teachers or administration. Parents are the child's best advocate. You can and should speak up on behalf of your children, and in the process gain the confidence, skills, and power to control the quality of life for your children and yourself.

BE THEIR MOTHER,
NOT THEIR SERVANT!

For most women motherhood evokes feelings of great joy as well as intense responsibility. These feelings often invoke an uneasy sense of inadequacy, especially in the new mother, as she tries to attend to the numerous needs of the newborn. The realization that everything she does or doesn't do, how she thinks and feels has some effect on her child, is often overwhelming. But, simultaneously, this inspires her to love and protect her child even more. Undoubtedly newborns require an inordinate amount of care, love, and attention. The more the mother enjoys responding to her baby's needs, the more he thrives and develops in a rewarding way. During this first phase of motherhood, most women enjoy being indispensable to their infant. Instinctively, however, they realize that by the end of the first year the baby will be trying to feed himself (perhaps a little sloppily), and by the second year he will be attempting to dress himself. For most mothers these events are very reassuring, and they anticipate them with pride, because these represent their baby's first steps in the long road to independence and self-reliance.

In contrast, there are a considerable number of women for whom motherhood fulfills their need to be needed. Their ego strength and sense of self-worth seems to be tied to their being indispensable, and thus in control. They equate "doing for their child" as solid evidence of their deep love and unqualified devotion. They justify their behavior with the belief that the more they attend and do for their child, the more secure and happy he will be. Thus they continue to indulge and cater to the infant with the result that he becomes more helpless, dependent, and demanding. The baby's inherent need for his mother's care precludes his discouraging this behavior, since he must depend on her judgment to develop appropriate skills that would assist him to discover his own capabilities.

As the child gets older and continues this dependency, these women become increasingly puzzled, disappointed, and angry. They cannot imagine why their child is querulous, demanding, difficult, and impossible to please. They fail to understand where they went wrong. They feel they have done, and are still doing, everything for the child and he shows no appreciation. Usually their rationale for this outcome is that the child must have been born with some inherent genetic defect that causes him to be unappreciative and uncooperative. They completely ignore their misguided input upon their child's development.

Unfortunately, children who have been overindulged, either by their mother or both parents, usually remain dependent and immature. They lack motivation, are usually underachievers in school, and as they become older are seldom satisfied with their occupation and are difficult employees. If they get married, they are quite demanding and self-serving as spouses. If they are male, they expect their wives to cater to them and are seldom able to cope with the realities of everyday life. If they are women, they tend to adopt the "princess" or "better than thou" attitude and expect their spouse to meet all their needs. Those who remain single tend to feel cheated, become chronic fault-finders, and are bored, unproductive people.

Grown-up, overindulged children seldom participate or involve themselves in community activities or causes. They rarely move toward, or establish, a definite goal. They seem to drift or depend on others and are usually uncooperative associates. Consequently many of these spoiled, demanding, and complaining children continue to live at home long after they have grown up. At this point their mothers usually complain about their selfishness, rudeness, helplessness, and general unpleasantness. Their mothers invariably feel disrespected, unappreciated, and helpless. They lack the courage, conviction, and initiative to put their children out of their home. They find themselves becoming progressively unhappy, and their self-respect dwindles. Increasing anger and self-hatred almost inevitably leads to depression. Unfortunately, depressed people usually fear being left alone, so they continue to harbor their adult child. Thus, this self-defeating and unhappy practice persists.

Another category of overindulgent parents comprises single or divorced and working mothers. For one reason or another they believe that they are guilty of denying or depriving their children of a good family life. In order to compensate for their feelings of guilt these parents not only work hard at their outside job but also come home and clean house, prepare meals, and chauffeur their children to sports, band practice, and other activities. Even when their children are old enough and capable of doing things on their own, these mothers continue to bake cookies for various activities, look after their teenagers' clothing, and shop for special items they have requested. No matter how exhausted they feel, they submit to this abuse because they fear being known as "bad" mothers. Thus this unhappy situation is perpetuated. They fail to realize that the more they indulge their children, the more their children will take them for granted. The belief persists that somehow their children have been short-changed and deprived, and it is their responsibility to compensate for that.

Still another group of overindulgent parents includes those who feel they were deprived as children. Consequently they want their children to grow up with all the advantages they were denied. These parents lack the realization that they grew up to be competent and capable adults because their own parents insisted that they accept responsibility for themselves early in life. They fail to perceive that their overprotected and indulged children cannot and probably never will achieve their level of self-reliance and competence. They feel that by being extra nice and meeting their children's every wish, they will be cared for in old age by their children. This is a fallacy, because these children not only grow up to be selfish adults but also are often incapable of providing for themselves.

It is extremely important then that parents avoid being servants to their children. The following guidelines can help prevent the unhappy consequences of this practice for both parents and children.

1. Be sure you support and encourage the child's earliest attempts to do for himself. Although you can perform the task more efficiently and quickly, let the child try to do it, so that he will know and feel the satisfaction and independence of accomplishment.

2. Do not substitute your ideas and fantasies when he is playing. You can make suggestions, but once he starts, let him work things out for himself. Of course if he comes to you for advice you can help him think it out, but generally, letting the child use his own imagination and ingenuity will result in his becoming more resourceful and independent.

3. Small children generally have a longer attention span than most parents think. Allow them time to work out a solution or solve a puzzle. This gives them a sense of pride and competency.

4. Temper tantrums can be a sign of an overindulged child who has been manipulated by his parents, or who has been thwarted in his ability to become self-reliant. It may also indicate that the child is receiving too many mixed messages from his parents that are creating confusion and anxiety.

5. Allow young children to be useful and to perform chores that are within their capability. They are often eager to help. This offers the parent an opportunity for genuine praise and increases the child's self-esteem.

6. Avoid extreme permissiveness. Every child needs limits and structure. These help the child to feel secure, protected, and loved. A child cannot and should not be his own parent. The overindulged, spoiled child is never happy even at home.

7. Chores should be assigned equally and fairly in terms of age and capability. The sex of the child should generally not be a factor in assigning tasks or privileges.

8. Praise and recognition are important aspects of parenting. These inspire high self-esteem and generate initiative. Even when the child's performance is not perfect, find something nice to say before you criticize.

9. If you have been your children's servant, begin to make changes as rapidly as possible. You may wish to make a list of chores and call a family meeting at which you request each member's cooperation. Give them a chance to volunteer for the various chores. Set up a system of rewards and consequences for what each child does or does not do. Consistent follow-up on your part ensures your commitment to them and to yourself, and helps the children to feel they are contributing members of the family.

10. If all fails, get help. The phenomenon of mother–servant and tyrant–child is quite prevalent. You may choose group, individual, or family counseling. Most communities have several resources, and the yellow pages in your phone book contain much helpful information in this regard. It is essential that your servant days are over so that your children will learn to cope, be self-reliant, and become happier, more independent and empathic human beings.

Based on "Are You Their Mother or Their Servant?" by Ellen Switzer. Family Circle Magaine, *May 19, 1978.*

Meeting 7
Industry vs. Inferiority

A. Greetings and opening remarks.
   1. Leader has participants check attendance sheet.
   2. Leader reviews previous meeting—fields questions and comments.
   3. Leader invites parents to describe impact of new methods on their children.
      a. "What is improving?"
      b. "What is going wrong?"
      c. "How are you feeling?"
   4. Discussion.
B. Topical presentation: Industry vs. inferiority—the sixth developmental stage.
C. Discussion highlights.
   1. Importance of parents' modeling behavior.
   2. Importance of structure and discipline in helping children to organize and develop a sense of adequacy.
   3. Encourage and praise children to do for themselves the things they are perfectly capable of doing.
   4. Role of fantasy and daydreaming—this can be constructive rather than destructive.
   5. Encourage positive socialization patterns.
   6. Importance of answering child's questions honestly.
   7. Parents should take a sincere interest in what their child is doing and why—without taking over. Praise and encouragement should be given freely.
   8. Significance of stimulation—trips, museums, family discussions, reasonable TV viewing, and so on, all encourage learning.
   9. Motivation evolves from a feeling of confidence, autonomy, and a sense of purpose. It is anchored in self-esteem.
D. Human relations training.
   1. Parents usually ask many questions on "How can I motivate my child?"
   2. Prevent overscheduling. Parents often need help in setting limits and in helping children schedule their own activities.
   3. Continuing role-playing, leader helps parents to arrive at their own solutions, to evolve reasonable alternatives, or a system of rewards or consequences. Emphasis is placed on teaching the child cause and effect to strengthen his sense of autonomy or inner control.

4. It is essential that the leader be empathic, genuine, and constructive during this process, so that parents can be empathic with their children.

E. Preparation for next meeting.
    1. Distribute handouts.

F. Suggested parent handouts for meeting 7A.
    1. Identity vs. Role Diffusion.
    2. Helping Children to Learn
    3. What's Good for Your Marriage Is Good for Your Children!
    4. Guidelines for Parenting

(*Note:* When dealing with parents of adolescents, the leader moves to stages 7A and 7B. Refer to supplementary meetings 7A and 7B.)

Background for topical presentation: School years are a period of slower physical growth, with steady development and emphasis on cognitive learning. A child's recognition in school is based on his productivity. He is learning to organize himself, things, facts, and the like; he is learning to differentiate, to discriminate, and to assimilate various concepts to relate them to his world.

This is the stage when good work habits, concentration, and application develop. The child tends to idealize the opposite sex parent and to identify with the parent of the same sex. He learns to form close peer friendships (usually with the same sex) and is finding out that "doing things" is fun. Confidence and self-esteem grow from productivity, recognition, approval from friends, teachers, and parents. This enables the child to develop his potential and to freely explore and dedicate himself to new and varied projects.

Lack of encouragement, praise, and appropriate recognition, and inability to organize himself or to attend to his work can result in an overall sense of inferiority or inadequacy. An "I can't" attitude and inability to complete tasks or commit himself to an idea or person may be evident. Homework is often unfinished or poorly done. Fearing failure, the child therefore finds "not doing" easier than "doing badly." In some cases the child may develop a perfectionistic stance in an effort to avoid failure; if he cannot do something perfectly—he will not attempt to do it at all.

INDUSTRY VS. INFERIORITY

Stage five represents the ages from six to eleven. These elementary school years are usually referred to as the latency phase. It is a time during which the child's love for the parent of the opposite sex and rivalry with the same sex parent are quiescent. It is also a period during which the child becomes capable of deductive reasoning, and of playing and learning according to rules. During this period children begin to understand how to play such games as checkers and other "take turn" activities that require obedience to rules. Erikson believes that the psychosocial dimension emerging during this period has a sense of industry at one extreme and a sense of inferiority at the other.

Industry is the dominant theme of this period. The child is concerned with *how* things are made, *how* they work, and *what* they do. It is the Robinson Crusoe age in the sense that the enthusiasm and minute detail with which Crusoe describes his activities appeals to the child's own budding sense of industry. When children are encouraged in their efforts to make, to do, or to build practical things (whether it be to construct creepy crawlers, tree houses, or airplane models; or to cook, bake, or sew); and when they are allowed to finish their products, and are praised and rewarded for their results, they have their sense of industry enhanced. Parents who see their children's efforts at making and doing as "mischief," or simply "making a mess" encourage poor work habits and a sense of inferiority in their children.

During these elementary school years, the child's world is expanding to include social institutions other than family. These play a central role in his development. A child's school experiences can affect the industry-vs.-inferiority balance. Because the school provides a wide range of subjects and interests, the child has the opportunity to discover his strengths and weaknesses. As the teacher praises and encourages his areas of competence, the child can learn to develop or accept his weaknesses without destroying his initiative and industry. Thus, the child whose sense of industry may not have been encouraged in his home now has the opportunity to have it revitalized by school activities and by the encouragement of sensitive and committed teachers and other adults with whom he comes in contact. Thus, the child's sense of industry or inferiority no longer depends solely on the caretaking efforts of the parents. It can be inspired and reinforced by the interest and actions of other significant adults.

Based on "Erik Erikson's Eight Ages of Man," by David Elkind. New York Times Magazine, 5 April 1970.

Raising Children

The results of a survey of parents whose children are considered successful and are now over age twenty-one implies there seems to be a common "parent sense" about effective parenting. Although the parents surveyed were mainly from traditional, two-parent families, parents in other circumstances can apply these guidelines to their own situations. For example, single parents or parents in families in which both spouses work may not have a lot of time to spend with their children, but the quality of the time spent—playing and talking with their children and doing things together as a family—is equally important. Similarly, while the parents who were surveyed emphasized the importance of a good marital relationship and the need to spend some time away from their children with their spouses, single parents can foster a healthy personal adjustment by arranging time to be alone or to participate in activities with other adults.

The most frequent responses of the parents are classified under ten basic principles about which there seems to be general agreement. Although not new, these principles of child rearing can offer a genuinely helpful guide to parents, teachers, day-care workers, and others who care for children.

Love Abundantly

The most important task is to love and really care about children. This not only gives children a sense of security, belonging, and support, but it also smooths out the rough edges of childhood. Parental love should be special in two respects.

Firstly, it should be constant and unconditional—which means it is always present, even when the child is acting in an unlovable manner. Secondly, parents should be open in expressing and showing love so that children are never uncertain about its presence. This means parents should hug and praise their children at every available opportunity.

Discipline Constructively

Discipline means setting and adhering to standards of behavior. After love, the parents stressed the importance of giving clear direction and enforcing limits on a child's behavior.

Discipline is an essential preparation for adjusting to the outside world; it makes a child better behaved and happier. It is best to use a positive approach by saying, "Do this," more often than "Don't do that." Be certain that you punish when you say you will. Be firm by "saying what you mean and meaning what you say." And punish as soon after the misdeed as possible; do not put an extra burden on Dad by saying, "Just wait until your father comes home."

Apart from firmness and immediacy, the parents described the following qualities of constructive discipline:

- *Be consistent:* Do not undermine the rules set by your spouse. Disagreements regarding childrearing must be resolved in privacy—never in front of the children.

- *Be clear:* Establish a few simple rules and spell them out clearly in advance. The child should never be confused about what the rules are.

- *Administer in private:* If possible, never punish a child in front of anyone. This tends to antagonize the child and he or she may continue to misbehave to save face.

- *Be reasonable and understanding:* Explain the reason why a child is being given directions: "The stove is hot, please keep away so you will not be burned." However, do not be afraid to say on occasion, "Do it because I say so." In addition, try to understand a child's point of view and meet him or her halfway. This will give you a closer relationship.

- *Be flexible:* With adolescents, bargaining is an effective tool. On occasion, it is good for both the parents and the child to be able to bend the rules a little. Also, what works with one child will not necessarily work with another. The child's individual personality enters into it.

- *Discourage continued dependency:* Try to give a child an ever-expanding role in making decisions affecting his or her life. As children reach adolescence, encourage independence, knowing that you have done all you could to form good behavior patterns.

- *Be authoritative:* If you are hesitant or indecisive, or if you feel guilty about disciplining children, you may not do a good job. Remember that you have years of experience, so stick to your decisions. Never let a child talk you out of a punishment you believe necessary. Have the courage to call on and trust your own common sense.

The parents also discussed the type of punishment they found most effective. They said that when a child hurts another person or destroys property, the child should apologize and, when necessary, make restitution from his or her own money. Sending children to their rooms or depriving them of something they enjoy doing was also considered to be a good punishment. Moreover, the parents generally agreed that spanking a young child (that is, a quick lick on the backside) was OK when necessary. They cautioned that a child should never be beaten, hit on the head, or hit as a means of satisfying parental anger. This finding agrees with most surveys which disclose that most parents (about 85 percent) report that they occasionally spank their children.

Spend Time Together

"Spend lots of time with your children!" was a frequent recommendation. The parents felt that this time should be spent in:

- *Playing:* Spend some time each day playing with the children. The sole purpose of this play should be enjoyment—not to influence them.

- *Talking together:* Have real conversations with kids—times when you both listen and sincerely react to one another.

- *Teaching:* Actively teach your children such work skills as cooking and car repair.

- *Encouraging family activities:* Family spirit and a sense of belonging are developed by doing things together as a family. Have regular family outings, special family dinners, and spend holidays together. Go to social, sporting, and religious events together. Conduct family council meetings and make decisions together. One parent recommended that families "reduce TV watching by playing family games or by playing musical instruments together." Another said, "You can't fool children by giving them things (toys, TV) rather than your time and attention."

Tend to Personal and Marital Needs

A number of parents specified that personal adjustment was an important first step to effective childrearing. One noted that to relate well to children, adults must be comfortable with themselves. Another parent said that one should not completely sacrifice oneself for the family but rather, "Keep part of yourself for yourself and do something you enjoy." By treating yourself well, this parent felt, you will avoid the feeling of being *mistreated*, used *unfairly*, or *overburdened* when something goes wrong. A sense of *humor* about one's faults and the misfortunes of life was also thought to be an important aspect of personal adjustment.

Love, respect, and faithfulness between spouses provide needed security to the family. Two comments by parents seem particularly helpful.

A household in which love is openly expressed is a household in which children flourish. Verbalizing love to one's children is not enough. Parents should make every effort to let their youngsters see warmth and tenderness in their marital relationship. Parents should not underestimate the importance of letting their children know how delighted they are when their spouses enter the house. The morning greeting and the goodnight kiss set an atmosphere which encourages the same kind of affection in the hearts and minds of the children.

A husband and wife are apt to be successful parents when they give their marriage the first priority. It may seem that the children are getting "second best" from this approach but they rarely are. A happy mother and father are most apt to have happy children when the children's roles are clearly and lovingly defined. Child-centered households produce neither happy marriages nor happy children.

These remarks highlight what many parents are reluctant to admit but what child experts are finding to be true: that children tend to detract from rather than enhance the closeness between husband and wife. Recent studies have shown that a couple's satisfaction with marriage and with each other tends to drop sharply just after their first child is born. With minor variations, it stays at a lower level during the childrearing years and only increases after the youngest child leaves home. Thus, the parents pointed out the need to work at maintaining closeness with a spouse by such things as weekends alone together, tender greetings, and thoughtful surprises.

Teach Right from Wrong

A number of responses highlighted the need for parents to actively teach children basic values and manners in order for them to get along well in society. Parents found the following ways helpful in socializing their children: the assignment of chores and other responsibilities at home; religious affiliation; insistence that the children treat others with kindness, respect, and honesty; emphasis on table manners and other social graces in the home; part-time jobs outside the home when the children were old enough; and the setting of personal examples of moral courage and integrity. The successful parents also stressed that they thought parents should clearly state their own moral values and discuss them with their children. Specific comments of parents include the following:

- "Children should be made aware of proper values—behavioral, financial, and so forth. When they stray, parents should communicate in a manner which encourages the child to listen—do not be permissive or rigid but firm, so the children know exactly where you stand."
- "Teach children to respect people, to be honest, and to treat others as they themselves would like to be treated."
- "All children have to be taught right from wrong, respect for others and their property, and for older people."
- "Teach them the value of truthfulness. Time and again I recall telling the children that if they told us the truth about a situation we would do all in our power to help them, for in knowing the real facts we could deal with any misstatements by others. If, however, they lied, we would be unable to be of much help because we couldn't depend on them."

Develop Mutual Respect

The parents emphasized the need to insist that all family members treat each other with respect. First of all, this means that parents should act in respectful ways to the children. The following behaviors exemplify this respect: politeness to children (saying "thank you" and "excuse me"); apologizing to a child when you are wrong; showing an active interest in the children's activities and TV shows; being honest and sincere with children at all times; not favoring one child in the family; following through on promises made; and showing basic trust in a child's character and judgment.

In addition, parents should insist on being treated in a respectful way by the children. If parents treat each other with respect and love, and teach the children to respect their parents, a solid foundation will be laid. Another parent suggested: "Parents should maintain their individuality and cultivate their own interests and talents. The time, feelings, and interests of both parents and children should be respected."

Really Listen

Parents should really listen to their child, from his or her earliest years—which means giving undivided attention, putting aside one's own thoughts and beliefs, and trying to understand the child's point of view. As one parent stated: "No matter how busy or involved you are, listen to your child as a person. Listening means understanding and communicating, not the physical act of hearing."

It also means talking your child's language, encouraging the expression of feelings—both good and bad—and allowing the child to show hostility or anger without fear of losing your love.

Offer Guidance

In offering guidance to children when they have problems, the parents recommended that you be brief—state your thoughts in a few sentences rather than make a speech. They also felt it is helpful to make children understand that, although your door is always open to discuss difficulties, before you will offer solutions you expect them to have thought about the problem and to have tried to come up with possible solutions themselves.

Other thoughts by parents on counseling children were:

- Don't force your opinions, likes, dislikes. Offer them strictly as your opinion, not as law.

- Forbidden fruit is always so tempting, so play it low-key with undesirable activities, TV shows, etc. Kids will usually respect your opinion if you are honest, and they will tend to follow your guidance unless they just have to "find out for themselves."

Independence

Recognizing that it is difficult to let children go, the parents advocated gradually allowing them more and more freedom or control over their own lives. By fostering independence you will gain their affection and their respect. Children should be given freedom to make decisions regarding minor matters first; then the areas of decision making should be expanded gradually.

The parents also observed that children have a continuing need for parental support and encouragement throughout adolescence and young adulthood. As one parent expressed it: "Once your children are old enough, kind of phase yourself out of the picture. But always be near when they need you."

Be Realistic

Developing realistic expectations about childrearing was also mentioned. Parents advised that one should expect to make mistakes and to realize that outside influences—such as peer group pressure—will increase as children mature. Parents reaffirmed the saying that childrearing is a series of "tough times and tender moments." One parent remarked: "Don't expect things to go well all the time. Childrearing has never been an easy job; it has its sorrows and heartaches but it also has its great joys and this is what makes it all worthwhile."

Parenting indeed is not a simple task, and it is easy to become confused and uncertain at times. The plain old-fashioned "parent sense" expressed here seems sensible and stable compared to the passing fads and theories.

The most important thing that parents in this study learned by experience is that steadfast love must go hand in hand with discipline; indeed, one is not truly possible without the other. Moreover, in order to love and discipline most effectively, it is necessary to spend constructive time with the children. It would seem, then, that while adjusting to changing times, it is important for parents to hold fast to these and other basic, unchanging principles of childrearing.

Plain Talk Series, Hilda Fried, editor. Division of Scientific and Public Information, National Institute of Mental Health.

THE ANGRY CHILD

Handling children's anger can be puzzling, draining, and distressing for adults. In fact, one of the major problems in dealing with anger in children is the angry feelings that are often stirred up in us. It has been said that we as parents, teachers, counselors, and administrators need to remind ourselves that we were not always taught how to deal with anger as a fact of life during our own childhood. We were led to believe that to be angry was to be bad, and we were often made to feel guilty for expressing anger.

It will be easier to deal with children's anger if we get rid of this notion. Our goal is not to repress or destroy angry feelings in children—or in ourselves—but rather to accept the feelings and to help channel and direct them to constructive ends.

Parents and teachers must allow children to feel all their feelings. Adult skills can then be directed toward showing children acceptable ways of expressing their feelings. Strong feelings cannot be denied, and angry outbursts should not always be viewed as a sign of serious problems; they should be recognized and treated with respect.

To respond effectively to overly aggressive behavior in children we need to have some ideas about what may have triggered an outburst. Anger may be a defense to avoid painful feelings; it may be associated with failure, low self-esteem, and feelings of isolation; or it may be related to anxiety about situations over which the child has no control.

Angry defiance may also be associated with feeligns of dependency, and anger may be associated with sadness and depression. In childhood, anger and sadness are very close to one another and it is important to remember that much of what an adult experiences as sadness is expressed by a child as anger.

Before we look at specific ways to manage aggressive and angry outbursts, several points should be highlighted:

- We should distinguish between anger and aggression. Anger is a temporary emotional state caused by frustration; aggression is often an attempt to hurt a person or to destroy property.

- Anger and aggression do not have to be dirty words. In other words, in looking at aggressive behavior in children, we must be careful to distinguish between behavior that indicates emotional problems and behavior that is normal.

In dealing with angry children, our actions should be motivated by the need to protect and to teach, not by a desire to punish. Parents and teachers should show a child that they accept his or her feelings, while suggesting other ways to express the feelings. An adult might say, for example, "Let me tell you what some children would do in a situation like this. . . ." It is not enough to tell children what behaviors we find unacceptable. We must teach them acceptable ways of coping. Also, ways must be found to communicate what we expect of them. Contrary to popular opinion, punishment is not the most effective way to communicate to children what we expect of them.

Responding to the Angry Child

Some of the following suggestions for dealing with the angry child were taken from *The Aggressive Child* by Fritz Redl and David Wineman. They should be considered helpful ideas and not be seen as a "bag of tricks."

Catch the child being good. Tell the child what behaviors please you. Respond to positive efforts and reinforce good behavior. An observing and sensitive parent will find countless opportunities during the day to make such comments as, "I like the way you come in for dinner without being reminded"; "I appreciate your hanging up your clothes even though you were in a hurry to get out to play"; "You were really patient while I was on the phone"; "I'm glad you shared your snack with your sister"; "I like the way you're able to think of others"; and "Thank you for telling the truth about what really happened."

Similarly, teachers can positively reinforce good behavior with statements like, "I know it was difficult for you to wait your turn, and I'm pleased that you could do it"; "Thanks for sitting in your seat quietly"; "You were thoughtful in offering to help Johnny with his spelling"; "You worked hard on that project, and I admire your effort."

Deliberately ignore inappropriate behavior that can be tolerated. This does not mean that you should ignore the child, just the behavior. The "ignoring" has to be planned and consistent. Even though this behavior may be tolerated, the child must recognize that it is inappropriate.

Provide physical outlets and other alternatives. It is important for children to have opportunities for physical exercise and movement, both at home and at school.

Manipulate the surroundings. Aggressive behavior can be encouraged by placing children in tough, tempting situations. We should try to plan the surroundings so that certain things are less apt to happen. Stop a "problem" activity and substitute, temporarily, a more desirable one. Sometimes rules and regulations, as well as physical space, may be too confining.

Use closeness and touching. Move physically closer to the child to curb his or her angry impulse. Young children are often calmed by having an adult nearby.

Express interest in the child's activities. Children naturally try to involve adults in what they are doing, and the adult is often annoyed at being bothered. Very young children (and children who are emotionally deprived) seem to need much more adult involvement in their interests. A child about to use a toy or tool in a destructive way is sometimes easily stopped by an adult who expresses interest in having it shown to him. An outburst from an older child struggling with a difficult reading selection can be prevented by a caring adult who moves near to say, "Show me which words are giving you trouble."

Be ready to show affection. Sometimes all that is needed for any angry child to regain control is a sudden hug or other impulsive show of affection. Children with serious emotional problems, however, may have trouble accepting affection.

Ease tension through humor. Kidding the child out of a temper tantrum or outburst offers the child an opportunity to "save face." However, it is important to distinguish between face-saving humor and sarcasm or teasing ridicule.

Appeal directly to the child. Tell him or her how you feel and ask for consideration. For example, a parent or a teacher may gain a child's cooperation by saying, "I know that noise you're making doesn't usually bother me, but today I've got a headache, so could you find something else you'd enjoy doing?"

Use physical restraint. Occasionally a child may lose control so completely that he has to be physically restrained or removed from the scene to prevent him from hurting himself or others. This may also "save face" for the child. Physical restraint or removal from the scene should not be viewed by the child as punishment but as a means of saying, "You can't do that." In such situations, an adult cannot afford to lose his or her temper, and unfriendly remarks by other children should not be tolerated.

Encourage children to see their strengths as well as their weaknesses. Help them to see that they can reach their goals.

Use promises and rewards. Promises of future pleasure can be used both to start and to stop behavior. This approach should not be compared with bribery. We must know what the child likes—what brings him pleasure—and we must deliver on our promises.

Say NO! Limits should be clearly explained and enforced. Children should be free to function within those limits.

Tell the child that you accept his or her angry feelings, but offer other suggestions for expressing them. Teach children to put their angry feelings into words, rather than fists.

Build a positive self-image. Encourge children to see themselves as valued and valuable people.

Use punishment cautiously. There is a fine line between punishment that is hostile toward a child and punishment that is educational.

Model appropriate behavior. Parents and teachers should be aware of the powerful influence of their actions on a child's or group's behavior.

Teach children to express themselves verbally. Talking helps a child have control and thus reduces acting out behavior. Encourage the child to say, for example, "I don't like your taking my pencil. I don't feel like sharing just now."

The Role of Discipline

Good discipline includes creating an atmosphere of quiet firmness, clarity, and conscientiousness, while using reasoning. Bad discipline involves punishment which is unduly harsh and inappropriate, and it is often associated with verbal ridicule and attacks on the child's integrity.

As one fourth-grade teacher put it: "One of the most important goals we strive for as parents, educators, and mental health professionals is to help children develop respect for themselves and others." While arriving at this goal takes years of patient practice, it is a vital process in which parents, teachers, and all caring adults can play a crucial and exciting role. In order to accomplish this, we must see children as worthy human beings and be sincere in dealing with them.

Adapted from "The Aggressive Child" by Luleen S. Anderson, Ph.D., which appeared in Children Today *(Jan.–Feb. 1978), published by the Children's Bureau, Department of Health, Education, and Welfare.*

FEELINGS OF GUILT

Smoldering within the labyrinth of the mind, unjustified, excessive guilt can sour our enjoyment of living, hobble our social and business lives, worry, dishearten, and humiliate us. It can cause fears and anxieties that, in turn, can bring on a whole galaxy of emotional ills, from chronic fatigue to such self-punishing conditions as sexual frigidity and drug addiction. Full-blown, needless guilt can erupt in a self-loathing so bitter that it can torment a person to the point of suicide.

Dr. Herbert M. Adler, associate professor of psychiatry at Hahnemann Medical College in Philadelphia, calls guilt "central" to human existence but adds: "When it runs amok inside, it can—quite literally—paralyze us, making us totally unable to function as human beings."

But if guilt has a bad side, it is crucial to understand that it has a good face, too. In its simplest form, it is the realization of the sorrow over having done something morally, socially, or ethically wrong. "Guilt itself is a desirable human emotion," says Dr. Sidney M. Jourard of the University of Florida, "in the sense that it enables us to recognize what we have done wrong, when we have violated our own consciences, and the mores of our society."

Adds Dr. Adler: "Most of us have been brought up to believe that all guilt is harmful, unnecessary, and should be eradicated. That's as wrong as saying all germs are bad. If we never felt guilt, we would not learn in school, do our job properly, obey traffic rules, perform exercises, feed and clothe our children, work for our families, have good relationships with loved ones or live in harmony within our communities or with one another. In short, guilt is our society's regulator."

Perhaps psychologist Allan Fromme of New York says it best: "Guilt feelings are an inevitable accompaniment of the development of our conscience." It is this internal bellwether, ringing out the difference between right and wrong, that is the key factor in all the guilt feelings humankind has experienced over the years, and ever will. Knowing how it works—whether it is justified or whether it has run psychologically off the track like a machine suddenly gone berserk—is crucial.

Nobody is born with a conscience. It does not come as standard equipment, like the survival instinct or sex drive. Dr. Sigmund Freud, father of psychiatry, said that babies are "notoriously amoral . . . they have no inhibitions against their pleasure-seeking impulses."

Conscience is planted into them like a seed into clean soil by an "external power"— the most important of which are parents, the first to put the beginnings of his moral sentry into a new human being. To parents falls the task of checking a child's impulses, teaching what is right and what is wrong, making a new member of society aware that he or she must live by its rules.

The demands of the society in which a child is reared also play an important role. So, too, do the traditions of race, nationality, and even a neighborhood, which can force him into what psychologists call norms of behavior.

We cannot see conscience change like the curves of our bodies, nor can a doctor view its outlines with any X-ray, but it grows and develops just the same as we learn by teaching, by example, and by immersion into a lifestyle.

And just as surely, guilt grows and develops when we disobey, or think we do, the rules we have absorbed and that we feel must be obeyed.

Violating our society's edicts, too, can bounce back as guilt feelings even if these edicts are outdated. A young high-school valedictorian from a small Ohio city, reared in an ethnic background that had strict taboos against unmarried sex, was uncomfortable with the more relaxed standards of his new college classmates. After six months of trying to conform to their lifestyle, he failed all his courses. Consultation with the school's psychiatrist disclosed the problem: His early teachings stayed with him and had convinced him he was committing a crime that deserved punishment, so, unconsciously, he chose to fail his classes.

Different cultures place their own imprints upon their people's consciences that, in turn, produce their own, home-grown varieties of guilt. In Japan, for instance, certain forms of behavior are believed to bring deep shame upon their perpetrators, causing them to "lose face." Thus a Japanese man or woman may feel tortured by guilt, driven even to suicide, by actions that a Westerner would hardly consider worrying about.

A fascinating illustration of the curious effect of society upon our feelings of guilt has just been revealed, perhaps unconsciously, by the actress Liv Ullman. In her recently published autobiography, *Changing*, she admits feeling guilty because she could not spend enough time with her growing daughter Linn, now ten. "There were so many demands from the outside," she said in an open letter to the child, "people who wanted part of that time which we should have had together."

She mentions no feelings of guilt, however, at having given birth to Linn out of wedlock during her five-year relationship with the film director Ingmar Bergman. Apparently, in the culture in which Liv was raised, the concept of a mother's responsibility to her children is deeply imbedded, while unmarried motherhood does not carry with it society's strong disapproval.

Some people feel guilt more strongly than others and for less reason. "Some children," explains Dr. Adler, "grow up being accused frequently and inappropriately by parents and family members of 'bad' actions. Shame is drilled into them continually for behavior that is not truly shameful.

"If a parent lays more of a guilt trip on a child than he can tolerate, the youngster tends to go in one of two directions. Unable to live with the guilt, he may rebel and find a refuge in drugs, delinquency, or other forms of antisocial behavior. Or the child may grow up loaded with a heavy burden of guilt, deeply convinced that he is a bad, undeserving person."

Then trouble—often serious trouble—can arise. Recently, researchers at the Duke University Medical Center in Durham, North Carolina, surveyed thirty-four persons who were admitted for attempting suicide. Of this number, twenty-six, or almost 80 percent, had past histories in which guilt—sometimes unconscious, sometimes not—played a prominent role. And according to Dr. Karl A. Menninger, one of the founders of the famed psychiatric clinic in Topeka, Kansas, and a noted authority on the reasons why people take their lives, "Suicide is a combination of hate, rage, revenge, a social guilt, and a feeling of unbearable frustration." In other words, intense feelings of guilt can often make life literally unbearable.

Investigators are learning that guilt also plays a significant part in suicide attempts by teenagers and even younger children. Dr. Reginald S. Louri, past president of the American Academy of Child Psychiatry, studied forty youngsters aged three to fourteen who had tried to take their own lives. After intensive interviews, he concluded that one in four were seeking to be punished either for masturbation or because they had wished themselves or someone else dead and could not live with the terrible thoughts.

Yet the influence of parents and other circles in which the child moves is only part of the story. The rest may live in the still-unlocked mysteries of the mind. Studies are showing that guilt will frequently mask wishes to atone in strange ways.

Accident-proneness, for instance, has been traced in some cases to a powerful emotional need to suffer for real or fancied misdeeds. Similarly, a person haunted by a sense of some inexplicable wrongdoing for which he feels an unbearable tension may "confess" to a crime he did not commit in order to receive the punishment he is convinced he deserves. And many experts believe that the tendency to absorb large doses of guilt may be inherited, like some forms of emotional illness. "Perhaps some day we might find the answer in the genes," says Dr. Adler.

Paradoxically, this baffling and often perverse emotion hits hardest at those with the least reason to be affected by it. In a classic study done some years ago, Harvard University psychologists asked subjects to solve twenty tough problems, placing next to each a booklet containing the answers. The subjects were told they could look at some solutions but not others, then were left alone in the exam room. At least they thought they were. Actually, the testers watched carefully through a one-way mirror.

Of the ninety-three persons tested, all college graduates, 46 percent violated orders and peeked; the rest did not. Later, all subjects were asked how they would feel if they had sneaked looks at the prohibited answers.

Fully 75 percent of those who broke the rules said their reaction would be calm indifference. But 84 percent of those who obeyed them replied they would have felt guilty, conscience-stricken, or ashamed!

And the latter replied so emphatically that the researchers reported they "could hardly escape the conviction that they were describing an emotion that they had often vividly experienced." In other words, the sterner your conscience, and the more vigilantly it monitors your thoughts and actions, the worse you will feel if you do something you think is wrong.

Clearly, then, knowing how to handle excessive and inappropriate guilt can help us avoid mental suffering, emotionally induced illness, and even tragedy. But sometimes powerful guilt feelings are pushed far beneath the layers of our conscious thinking. In such cases, professional help may be needed to bring them to the surface. Only then, points out

Dr. Jourard, can an individual evaluate the validity of his or her guilt reaction and thus attempt to alter it.

How can you learn to penetrate guilt's many disguises? First take a long inward look, seeking the core reason for your feelings. Are you tense because of something you did or failed to do? Have you broken, or thought you have, some deeply held moral or ethical precept? Have you lied, cheated, broken a promise, violated some taboo, hurt somebody? Are you hiding a secret you feel should be told to somebody dear to you?

Next, learn the difference between the rightful and the unreasonable expectations you have of yourself. The individual should ask two key questions, declares Dr. Michael Petite, assistant professor of psychiatry at Georgetown University Medical Center in Washington, D.C., "Why do I feel guilty?" is one, and "Should I feel guilty?" is the other.

At this point, Dr. Petite says, reappraise all the rules that have been set down for you during your lifetime. Take a whole new look at the principles, not created by yourself, but prescribed by parents, friends, society, and others.

"Develop mind muscle as you sort them out and judge them," says Dr. Petite. "Are they sound, sensible precepts that you believe in, or unwarranted and even foolish? Are those taboos you have always been convinced were bad really so dreadful after all? Most important, are those principles realistic and valid for you at your stage of life and relevant in the society in which you now live and work?"

Often, woefully wrong teachings in early childhood remain with us for years, hobbling our behavior. A young husband loved his wife but would seldom kiss her. Understandably, she read his refusal to kiss as a lack of love, and her resentment grew. Yet the answer was simple: years before, he had been taught by his mother that kissing was immoral. Even though intellectually he no longer accepted the view, he was unable to rid himself of the guilt until he could recognize its cause.

Masturbation, harshly disapproved by many parents, is a prime guilt-producer in adulthood. Sexual authorities point out that the practice is not only one of the normal experiences of growing up but hardly abnormal or shameful in adulthood either. Yet many widowed or divorced persons suffer needlessly because of the taboo branded onto them early in life. Dr. Mary S. Calderone, president of the Sex Information and Education Council of the United States declares that masturbation on the part of the formerly married person with normal sexual desires "fulfills a necessary function." The individual, she says, "must . . . recognize that his or her needs and desires are not abnormal but are part of the everyday behavior of human beings everywhere. He or she must be able to choose maturely a method for meeting these sexual needs and to accept the choice of method in a mature fashion."

Here are some other guidelines to help you distinguish between the reasonable and unreasonable demands you might be making on yourself:

You cannot hope to remain patient and even-tempered toward those you love. "Countless people torment themselves needlessly," declares Dr. Adler, "because they feel hostile and resentful at times toward their children, parents, wives, and husbands. Their guilt mounts as they tell themselves: 'I must be a bad person to feel this way and there must be something terribly wrong with me.' They aren't and there isn't. For anger directed at those we love is not only normal but inevitable. As long as we can control our anger or discharge it harmlessly, we should not look upon ourselves as unfit parents, children or mates."

Your responsibilities to aging parents may be fewer than you are imposing upon yourself. Guilt resulting from "neglect" of parents is a cliché, the subject of comedians' jokes and at least one bestseller, *Portnoy's Complaint*. Dr. Petite explains that many aging parents, out of the self-centeredness that develops with increasing years, use this guilt to keep their ties with their children closebinding. Likewise, few young couples escape the anguish that results from being unable to give their parents as much time and attention as they did in earlier years.

Although it is hard for aging parents to accept the fact that their children do not need them as they once did, those who insist upon daily visits and other constant attentions must be shown that their attitudes may be unreasonable, says Dr. Petite.

Do what is right for you. The rise of feminism, which is supposed to offer women alternatives, not take them away, has had an unusual backfiring effect: Countless women now feel guilt because they are not in paying, prestigious jobs or working toward them. An organization called the Martha Movement is seeking to ease this collective guilt by reaffirming the value of homemaking as a form of lifework and promoting the idea that women should be able to choose the life that suits them.

Perfection is an unattainable ideal. Mistakes will happen, must happen. Berating yourself for errors on the job or at home is useless exercise. Joseph P. Kennedy, father of the late president, had a reputation for pushing his nine children to win, but he also told them never to feel badly if they tried and failed. "Once you've done your best," he said many times, "the hell with it." It is still good advice.

If you have done something morally or ethically wrong, accept it—and forget it. Apologize if you can, correct the misdeed in whatever way is proper. Say nothing if you will hurt someone else grievously, recognizing that "telling all" is actually asking for punishment to ease your sense of guilt. "One can feel sorry about something without feeling guilty," said the late psychiatrist Dr. Theodor Reik. "A clear understanding of the significance of our misdeeds is emotionally healthier than hopeless misery afterward." Tell yourself if you have done it, that it was wrong—and that it is behind you.

Guilt is a civilizing force which when unbridled can cause much hurt. But with wisdom fortified by knowledge, this pervasive emotion can be tamed and used to your advantage as you go on with the business of living.

Plain Talk Series, Hilda Fried, editor. Division of Scientific and Public Information, National Institute of Mental Health.

STRESS

Dr. Hans Selye states that the physical reaction of the body stress is basically the same, regardless of whether the stressor is pleasant or unpleasant. He feels that the only complete freedom from stress is death. Humans thrive on stress because it makes life more interesting.

No matter what you are doing, you are under some amount of stress. Even in sleep your body must continue to function and react to the stress imposed by dreaming. Stress comes from two basic forces—the stress of physical activity and the stress of mental or emotional activity. It is interesting to note that stress from emotional frustration is more likely to produce disease, such as ulcers, than stress from physical work or exercise. In fact, physical exercise can relax you and help you deal with mental stress.

A type of stress that can be harmful is called *distress* which causes us to constantly readjust or adapt. For example, having a job you do not like can be constantly frustrating, and frustration is "bad" stress. Over time, it can result in fatigue, exhaustion, and even physical or mental breakdown. The best way to avoid it is to choose an environment that allows you to do the activities you enjoy that are meaningful to you. Your friends, your work, and even your future mate can be sources of challenging good stress or harmful distress.

However, the absence of work is not necessarily a way to avoid stress. Boredom can become an enemy capable of causing tremendous distress. Work is actually good for you as long as you can achieve something by doing it. It will only wear you out if it becomes frustrating because of failure or a lack of purpose.

To avoid distress, you should work at something (1) you are capable of doing; (2) you really enjoy; and (3) other people appreciate.

Body Reactions to Stress

Regardless of the source of stress, your body has a three-stage reaction to it: stage 1: alarm; stage 2: resistance; and stage 3: exhaustion.

In the alarm stage, the body recognizes the stressor and prepares for fight or flight. It releases hormones from the endocrine glands, which cause an increase in heartbeat and respiration, elevation in blood sugar level, increase in perspiration, dilated pupils, and slowed digestion. You will then choose whether to use this burst of energy to fight or flee.

In the resistance stage, the body repairs any damage caused from the stress. If, however, the stressor does not go away, the body cannot repair the damage and must remain alert.

This plunges you into the third stage—exhaustion. If this continues long enough, you may develop one of the "diseases of stress," such as migraine headaches, heart irregularity, or even mental illness. Continued exposure to stress during the exhaustion stage causes the body to run out of energy, and may even stop bodily functions. Since you cannot build a life completely free from stress or even distress, it is important that you develop some ways of dealing with stress.

Getting a Handle on Stress and Distress

1. *Work off stress.* If you are angry or upset, try to blow off steam physically by activities such as running, playing tennis, or gardening. Even taking a walk can help. Physical activity allows you a "fight" outlet for mental stress.

2. *Talk out your worries.* It helps to share worries with someone you trust and respect. This may be a friend, family member, clergyman, teacher, or counselor. Another person can help you see a new side to your problem and thus, a new solution. When you find yourself being preoccupied with emotional problems, it is wise to seek a professional listener, like a guidance counselor or psychologist. This is not admitting defeat. It is admitting you are an intelligent human being who knows when to ask for assistance.

3. *Learn to accept what you cannot change.* If the problem is beyond your control at this time, try your best to accept it until you can change it. It beats spinning your wheels, and getting nowhere.

4. *Avoid self-medication.* Although there are many chemicals, including alcohol, that can mask stress symptoms, they do not help you adjust to the stress itself. Many are habit-forming, so the decision to use them should belong to your doctor. It is a form of flight reaction that can cause more stress than it solves. The ability to handle stress comes from within you, not from the outside.

5. *Get enough sleep and rest.* Lack of sleep can lessen your ability to deal with stress by making you more irritable. Most people need at least seven to eight hours of sleep out of every twenty-four. If stress repeatedly prevents you from sleeping, you should inform your doctor.

6. *Balance work and recreation.* "All work and no play can make you a nervous wreck." Schedule time for recreation to relax your mind. Although inactivity can cause boredom, a little loafing can ease stress. This should not be a constant escape, but occasionally, you deserve a break.

7. *Do something for others.* Sometimes when you are distressed, you concentrate too much on yourself and your situation. When this happens, it is often wise to do something for someone else, and get your mind off of yourself. There is an extra bonus in this technique—it helps make friends.

8. *Take one thing at a time.* It is defeating to tackle all your tasks at once. Instead, set some aside and work on the most urgent.

9. *Give in once in awhile.* If you find the source of your stress is other people, try giving in instead of fighting and insisting you are always right. You may find that others will begin to give in, too.

10. *Make yourself available.* When you are bored and feel left out, go where the action is! Sitting alone will just make you more frustrated. Instead of withdrawing and feeling sorry for yourself, get involved. Is there a play or musical coming up? Chances are they will need help backstage. Get yourself back there and somebody will probably hand you a hammer or paint brush.

Recognizing stress as an ongoing part of life may well be the first step in dealing with it. Turn stress into a positive force and let it make life more interesting.

Plain Talk Series, Hilda Fried, editor. Division of Scientific and Public Information, National Institute of Mental Health.

Excerpts reprinted with permission from General Learning Corporation, Northbrook, Ill.

Supplementary Meeting 7A
For Parents of Adolescents

A. Greetings and opening remarks.
   1. Participants check attendance sheet.
   2. Leader reviews previous meeting and invites comments.
B. Human relations training—exercises.
   1. Discussion by participants on the relationship between themselves and their own parents, as well as on what they felt their parents expected from them.
      a. Leader invites parents to break up into small groups of approximately three to four persons. Each group will choose a recorder.
      b. The groups should discuss and respond to the following questions over a five-minute interval:
         i. Think back to when you were in high school and describe the relationship between yourself and your parents.
         ii. Compare the values you had with those of your parents (that is, points of agreement or disagreement).
         iii. How would your parents have described you?
         iv. Identify your parents' expectations of you at that time.
      c. Recorder will report group's responses to all participants.
      d. Leader highlights similarities and differences.
      e. Leader highlights expectations of their parents and invites comments on how these compare with what they are expecting of their own teenagers.
      f. Discussion will be quite animated.
   2. Discussion on how their teenagers perceive them as parents and the expectations they have of their children.
      a. Group reconvenes into smaller groups with same recorder. Leader requests that they now:
         i. Identify how they think their teenagers perceive them.
         ii. Identify how their teenagers think the parents see them.
         iii. Discuss the expectations that their teenagers think the parents have of them.
      b. Leader requests recorder to report findings.
      c. Group discusses their findings.

        d.   Leader reflects on their perceptions and feelings, and clarifies and synthesizes discussion.

C. Topical presentation: Identity vs. role diffusion.

D. Discussion highlights.

    1.   Identity must be validated by others and it is essential to one's ability to make adult decisions (that is, career, choice of life-style, marriage partner).

    2.   Adolescence is a period of rapid emotional, physical, and social change. The child needs to adjust and adapt to the many changes incurred.

    3.   Being against something is a great need. By contrasting themselves and their ideas with opposite groups they firm up sense of self.

    4.   The adolescent talks things over endlessly with peers—this ends when lasting commitment is made.

    5.   Play as a major ego function recedes in importance, replaced by capacity for fantasy—rituals of gang or group behavior; chooses trust-inspiring persons as models.

    6.   Parents' role as the essential supports and value givers diminishes. Peers absorb most of prevailing social interest and energy.

    7.   Despite apparent discrepancies between youths' standards and aims and those of society, adolescents do not deviate too far from social norms. The individual slowly moves into society as an interdependent member. He searches for something and somebody to be true.

E. Preparation for next meeting.

    1.   Distribute handouts.

F. Suggested parent handouts for meeting 7B.

    1.   Intimacy vs. Isolation

    2.   Are Your Expectations of Your Children Realistic?

    3.   Good Study Tips

    4.   Helping Children Make Career Plans

    5.   Sexuality and Your Teenager

    6.   At Home with Your Teenager

Background for topical presentation: Identity is the feeling of knowing oneself in terms of self-knowledge and the ability to accept, respect, and like oneself and what one is becoming. Identity implies a certain mastery of the earlier childhood tasks and a readiness to face the challenge of the adult world as a potential equal. Identity is essential for making adult decisions (for example, career choice, choice of life-style, marriage partner, and so on).

The youth now strives toward integrating his inner and outer directions—what to be and in what context can he be and become. *"I ain't what I ought to be, I ain't what I'm going to be, but I ain't what I was!"* The young adult experiences rapid physical and psychological growth. Because of these changes his previous trust in his body and his mastery of its functions are being shaken. As he gradually regains these, he seeks constant reassurance from the peer group—who are also experiencing similar maturational changes, which generally upset the balance between the id, the ego, and the super-ego. Fortunately, the balance is ultimately restored as the adolescent integrates new feelings, perceptions and insights. It is a period of self-standardization in search of sexual age and occupational identity!

In order to fulfill his identity he must separate from his parents and move toward the peer group almost in total opposition to all he has known and been!

The adolescent requires time, understanding, and emotional support to integrate himself into adulthood. Adolescents need to work on the following areas in the developmental continuum:

- *Time perspective vs. time diffusion.* The concept of time is essential to identity. Only when he can see his life in perspective does his sense of time lead to a sense of full identity.

- *Self-confidence vs. apathy.* This involves a conflict between identity consciousness and escape into apathy. When his self-awareness and the impressions he conveys to others coincide, he can be certain of his own identity. On the other hand, self-consciousness, doubt, and confusion about himself cause his autonomy to recede.

- *Role experimentation vs. negative identity.* Positive or negative identity depends upon successful experimentation with a wide range of roles.

- *Anticipation of achievement vs. work paralysis.* The adolescent applies his sense of industry persistently in preference to unrelated situational opportunities; persistence and integration are essential to occupational identity and long-range plans.

- *Sexual identity vs. bisexual diffusion.* He must feel comfortable with members of opposite sex, needs to see self as wholly male/female; situations and attitudes for experimentation need resolution so that his sexual identity can adapt to the behavior currently expected of adults of his sex.

- *Leadership polarization vs. authority diffusion.* The adolescent selects his basic ideology, philosophy, or religion to provide an anchor of trust in life and in society; many choices are offered.

IDENTITY VS. ROLE DIFFUSION

Adolescence begins with puberty. This physical phenomenon—initiating the first menses in girls and the first seminal emission in boys—takes place over a period of several years. Typically this happens earlier with girls than with boys. Body growth and rapid chemical and psychological changes accompany puberty, and cause much puzzlement and wide mood swings that upset both child and parent.

The adolescent's world suddenly expands its physical, social, and emotional parameters. She deals more deeply with verbal and written information—leading to more mature mental development. With such expanded life spaces the adolescent is able to gather more facts and synthesize them into conscious generalizations that lead to abstract thinking.

Socially she goes through radical changes as well. Psychosexual drive demands her full attention and she tries to experience her *identity* through new and more satisfactory relationships outside her family. This is a period when youngsters find themselves growing away from their parents as they establish increasing independence and maturity. For the parents it is a time of letting go—of putting mutuality of love and honest communication to a severe test as they watch their child being influenced more by the peer group than by their upbringing! In the process of trying to establish herself as an individual, the adolescent rejects her parents and will often feel confused and guilty about her emotions. In testing other life-styles she finds herself disagreeing and growing away from the familiar pattern of her past home life. For both parents and adolescents emotional battles severely test the strength of family ties.

When parents are able to permit the teenager to achieve mastery of herself, and to find her own solutions in new and different situations; when they can remain supportive, yet honestly maintain a consistent value structure that the adolescent can respect and trust—then the youngster will grow into young adulthood with strong family ties and sense of personal identity. The adolescent ultimately evolves her own moral concepts and code of ethics, which usually are not too far removed from those of her parents.

In addition, the adolescent wants to be treated as a person in her own right, even when she is not quite sure of who or what she is becoming. She wants adults in whom she can confide and respect, and who honestly understand her problems as she seeks their solution. Most of all, she values adults who are loving, supportive, and sensitive, and who model (rather than preach) their beliefs!

As she establishes and solidifies her social relationships she is also learning about the realistic world of work. She uses her initiative and identity to explore occupations and her own inherent disposition to their demands. Deciding what one wants to be in life is largely a matter of defining one's identity and recognizing the emotional needs that the ultimate career selection can gratify. Thus, adolescents have an enormous number of decisions facing them. How they resolve these reveals their true identity.

Helping Children To Learn

How much you can help your child to learn depends upon your temperament, time available, and your interest in his progress. Here are some tips that can help you and your child.

1. *Provide time, place, and support.* You and your child should agree on a time and place for him to do his homework. Avoid interruptions or distractions such as TV, telephone, record playing, or munching. Even those children who are too young for homework should have a regular time and place for reading.

2. *Do not do his homework for him.* Be willing to discuss an assignment and help him to think through a problem. When you go over his homework you may question something you feel is wrong, but let him discover *why* it might be wrong, and how *he* can correct it. Do not get involved in an argument. Just making sure he knows his assignments, and does them, is enough for most children.

3. *Help him understand basic operations.* Building-block skills such as multiplication tables, vocabulary or spelling can be reviewed with him. You can listen and review basic skills, or dictate spelling words, but let him correct his own errors. Be sure he understands why things are done in a certain way.

4. *Monitor school performance.* Do not wait for the teacher to write you a note before you inquire how your child performs in school. In most areas minimum competency requirements have been established. For example, by the end of grade two, a child should be able to identify the main idea of a short paragraph; and by the end of third grade he should be able to do basic multiplication through five and nine. As a parent you should be aware of your child's progress, or whatever difficulties he may be experiencing in school. Most teachers are eager to send home assignments related to his area of difficulty, which can provide him with extra practice he can do at home.

5. *Stimulate your child.*

- Demonstrating the relationship between what he learns in school to daily life experiences.

- Have the young child read signs.

- When purchasing gas ask the child to calculate the cost for six to ten gallons—or whatever you are purchasing.

- To improve his writing, encourage him to write notes to grandparents, or friends, or to make shopping lists, or to write out whatever schedule he has planned for the day or week.
- Encourage him to discuss things of interest, or tell about a field trip he may have had, or an experience on the playground.
- Ask him to describe objects verbally—what he likes or does not like.
- Assist him in his ability to make judgments by asking him his reasons for liking or not liking a story; or a place he went to; or a movie; or a TV show.
- Encourage conversation at the dinner table and be sure you use the proper names for articles, foods, clothing, and so on.

The home has a continuous responsibility for a child's education that does not end when the child enters first grade. Parents can do a great deal to help the child understand that education is relevant to daily life and that it is a continuous process that can enrich our lives.

WHAT'S GOOD FOR YOUR MARRIAGE
IS GOOD FOR YOUR CHILDREN!

The quality of the interpersonal relationship between two parents often is reflected in the behavior, attitudes, and achievements of their children. Curiously enough many of the essential elements that contribute to the success of the marriage are equally important in establishing a positive relationship between parents and children. The very same dynamic factors that contribute to the well-being of husband and wife affect the interpersonal relationship between parents and children, and affects the child's developing personality in subtle and various ways. A good relationship between parents not only provides a loving, stable, and consistent environment for their children, but also can act as their model of how marriage really works.

The significant factors identified as vital elements of a good marriage (as well as affecting the children) are as follows.

1. *Being physically present.* Though this may seem a simplistic factor in making marriage work, frequent absences of one partner or another contribute greatly to the break-up of many marriages. Modern life makes many and numerous demands on adults and provides "good reasons" for being away from home. Nevertheless, a marriage can be seriously weakened when the principals do not establish a special and regular time to be together.

Both partners need to make this a priority to avoid the danger of becoming casual housemates who use the home as a hotel. No "right" amount of time can be prescribed, but when family members are apart more than they are together (other than during work hours) a sense of emotional distance results that precludes interchange of feelings, ideas, and discussion. Children particularly sense the absence of parents and often construe it as rejection. They tend to feel insecure and anchorless. The consistency of parental presence provides them with a sense of security and stability that makes the house feel like a home.

2. *Talking and sharing feelings and ideas.* A recent study discovered that the average couple spends about ten minutes a day in conversation. Obviously this cannot be construed as communication. Talking is more than exchanging information about the weather, the children, or the day's problems. It includes allowing your partner to know where you are emotionally, physically, and intellectually. It also means taking the time to listen and to

hear what your partner has on his or her mind. Too many partners communicate only at dinner, during TV commercials, or when they have company. Just because two people live together does not mean that they will know everything about each other by osmosis.

It takes interest and concern about each other, and time allotted for talking about feelings, ideas, dreams, and even disappointments. Children, too, need to spill out their experiences to trusting and loving adults. They need to know where parents stand on various issues and how they feel. They need validation and support for their feelings and ideas. If discussion is not permitted children feel unimportant and this can contribute to a lack of self-esteem.

3. *Listening and hearing.* Real listening is a creative act. It means understanding the unspoken language of the eyes, the stance of the body, and the feelings behind the words and tone of voice. One cannot listen and simultaneously be reading a newspaper or magazine. Listening cannot be faked. It requires giving the speaker your entire attention, interest, and concentration. Listening with empathy reassures your partner and makes her/him feel worthwhile. This applies to both children and adults. Listening in a bored and perfunctory manner often incites feelings of rejection and anger, which tends to decrease the child's self-esteem. Attending to what the child is saying and meaning helps her to feel like a worthwhile individual, accepted for herself, her ideas and what she is becoming.

4. *Touching and stroking.* Some couples find it difficult to express affection by touching, sitting close, holding hands, or holding each other during stress. With many couples physical contact occurs only during sex. When a couple avoids physical contact in a loving way, other than sex, they often feel used. Foreplay should not begin five minutes before having sex. In fact, it includes everything that happens before actually going to bed, and especially one's attitude and frame of mind. Touching can provide reassurance and security in a world filled with stress, indifference, and transience. Similarly, stroking, holding, or hugging your child makes her feel secure and wanted in a socially approved fashion.

5. *Empathizing.* The ability to feel for, and with whatever your partner is saying, feeling, and doing takes deep respect for her as a person, and an understanding of where she is at. Her awareness that the one she loves really cares and knows how she feels promotes a sense of unity and belonging that certainly strengthens the marriage. Empathy requires an ability to project yourself totally into your partner's feelings and experience so that you can perceive her from her point of view. Only when you can genuinely share the meaning of his or her experience as he or she perceives it can you comment, advise, or sympathize in a manner that will be both constructive and comforting. Likewise, being able to empathize with your children sensitizes them to the feelings and values of others, and helps to make them more responsible.

6. *Sexual compatibility.* Sex in marriage may be regarded as a microcosm of the entire relationship. Our emotions are too much a part of us and are reflected in the sex act. Any anger, guilt, resentment, or other emotions we may be feeling will affect our sexual response. Sexual problems can seldom be resolved through a sex manual. They usually relate to emotional hang-ups in our daily lives. To achieve sexual maturity and satisfaction a couple must evaluate and confront whatever problems exist in their overall relationship. Though sexual compatibility may not seemingly apply to a child's upbringing in the same sense as it does to the marriage, it is a well-known fact that children derive their sexual attitudes from the relationship they observe between their parents. These

attitudes and values persist well into their adulthood, eventually affecting their ability to be intimate with their own partners.

7. *Commitment.* Commitment supersedes all other requirements of a good marriage. Lately this concept seems to have been weakened, which in many cases accounts for the increase in the divorce rate. To commit one's self implies giving to the marriage totally and without reservation, all that one is, has, and does. If marriage is to be secure and lasting, one cannot enter into it on the basis of "if it works out." A deep personal commitment to confront and work out problems, to honestly recognize and resolve the inevitable differences, to help each other grow and become whatever each can be, and to make the marriage work for both partners, is the cornerstone of a successful and fulfilling relationship. Being able to commit oneself to someone, something, or to some cause is based on the development of autonomy, or the sense of having some control over one's life. This is learned very early and is modeled by the parents' own commitment to each other and to the child. What better gift can parents bestow upon themselves and their growing children?

8. *Enrichment.* Partners in a marriage can enrich each other by sharing their unique personality, gifts, imagination, ingenuity, and retinue of freinds. Enrichment can be derived from sharing a favorite vacation spot, developing a hidden talent, achieving a long- or short-term goal, or sharing ideas, books, music, or experiences. A happy, optimistic, and secure person can give a lot more to a marriage than one who is gloomy, fearful, pessimistic, and unhappy. Helping each other grow to one's fullest potential by doing things that result in happy memories will enrich the marriage and provide it with renewed vitality and enthusiasm. As guides and mentors to our children we can enrich them and ourselves by sharing our past and present worlds with them and yet allow them to experience their world in their own way. The things we do with them are what they will remember when, as mature adults, they think of "home."

Based on "What Every Good Marriage Needs," by Dr. I. Ralph Hyatt. Family Circle Magazine, *3 February 1978.*

GUIDELINES FOR PARENTING

1. *Provide emotional security.* Children need to feel unconditionally loved by their parents. Show affection freely in your own way. Let them know they can depend on your understanding and support even when they misbehave. Unacceptable behavior should be corrected with love.

2. *Deal with children honestly.* Always tell them the truth, and do your best to keep your promises. When you do not know the answer to their questions admit it, and offer to help them find the answer. Otherwise, children will eventually find out that you did not respect them enough to be honest with them. This will decrease their ability to trust you, themselves, and other adults.

3. *Discipline firmly, fairly, and consistently.* Most children need and want to be disciplined and be guided in adjusting to life situations. Discipline should be neither harsh, nor easy—but appropriate to the offense. Punishment or consequences should not depend upon the mood of the parents. Their purpose should be to teach the child fairness and socially acceptable behavior. Both parents should be in agreement about how and what will be punished. Remember that praise and reward are very effective methods of achieving good discipline, and should be used liberally.

4. *Rules should be clear, simple, and fair.* Establish rules in accordance to the values important to you. Be consistent in enforcing them. Children should know in advance the consequence of breaking the rules. Stick to the important ones. Avoid long lists of rules that make enforcement unwieldy and meaningless.

5. *Avoid intense or loud disagreements with your spouse in the presence of your children.* Some controversy or disagreements are normal in most marriages. However, severe and constant expression of hostility between parents creates anxiety, guilt, and feelings of insecurity in children. However, divergent issues that are discussed fairly can help children to realize that honest differences need not result in hostility.

6. *Encourage your child's emerging independence.* Provide opportunities that allow children to take responsibility and make decisions for themselves. Avoid doing things for him that he can do for himself. Being overprotective infantilizes children and makes them fearful of taking responsibility for themselves. Allowing him to work through some of his own problems increases his sense of competency, autonomy, and initiative, and makes him a happier, self-reliant individual.

7. *Provide appropriate and adequate sex education.* When children ask about sex respond calmly, honestly, and accurately, in language they can understand. Tell them as much as they want to know at that particular time—no more—no less. Be sure you do not embarrass or shame them. Try to deal with the facts of life in the context of their own readiness.

8. *Be aware of individual differences.* No two children, even in the same family, are alike. Children develop differently and at their own rate physically, emotionally, intellectually, and socially. Avoid forcing or pressuring them to conform to some preconceived pattern of development. Let them grow at their own rate in their own way. Individuation helps children to develop self-esteem and self-respect.

9. *Avoid making academic achievement their only reason for living.* Help your child to realize that learning is part of growing, that it can be fun and that it takes place out of school as well as in the classroom. Motivate him to learn by stimulating his interest in a wide range of activities. Emphasize knowledge and develop good study habits by teaching him organization and good work habits.

10. *Give your child a faith to live by.* In an age of tension, uncertainty, and doubts, a good sense of ethics and values, or a religion your child can believe in, is important. During times of stress, when even loved ones can offer little comfort, a sense of faith and trust can give him the courage to persevere and to believe in himself and to reach out to others.

Supplementary Meeting 7B
For Parents of Adolescents

A. Greetings and opening remarks.
   1. Parents check attendance sheet.
   2. Review previous week's meeting.
   3. Leader invites questions and comments.
B. Topical presentation: Intimacy vs. isolation.
C. Discussion highlights.
   1. Ego identity requires self-knowledge and strength of character when a person mates with another whose ego identity is complementary in some essential point.
   2. Commitment to mutual intimacy requires psychological readiness and maturity.
   3. Mutual trust, willingness to share, and an ability to care are essential for each partner's full and self-satisfying participation in society.
   4. Solidarity of marriage—an evolutionary and individual achievement of the selectivity of sexual love that can result in a sense of shared identity and mutual verification—is the finding of oneself as one loses oneself in another.
   5. In work and in marriage, career efforts are directed toward improving cooperation, making allowances for competition, and for friendships and other associations.
   6. Selection of occupation demands and depends on self-knowledge and self-esteem.
   7. Individual demonstrates capacity to love and to work—career choice is best when it can respond to inner needs of individual.
   8. Counterdevelopment at this stage results in a sense of isolation and distance, infused with feelings of social emptiness—sexuality may become superficial, meaningless, or even exploitive.
   9. Parents' relationship with each other provides powerful model.
   10. Love and nurturance provided by parents enable young adult to love herself with mate of her choice.
D. Human relations training.
   1. Leader uses questions or statements to encourage discussion and use role-playing.
   2. Sample lead statements:
      a. "Your son is a senior with good grades but has no idea of what he wants to do—and you feel he doesn't care."

  b. "You're really worried about your sixteen-year-old because she seems to be boy crazy."

  c. "You're wondering what you should say when your daughter wants to go on the 'pill.' "

  d. "You feel your son is experimenting with drugs but you don't know how to deal with it."

  e. "Your teenager thinks you're hopelessly out of date because you won't let her go away with her boyfriend for the weekend."

  f. "Your fourteen-year-old wants to stay out with her group beyond 10:30 p.m.

  g. "Your teenager worries you because she's never asked you any questions regarding sex."

  h. "Your daughter threatens to run away and you find it hard to handle her."

  i. "Your son's grades have dropped and he doesn't seem to go anywhere or do anything—so you're really worried because he won't talk about it."

E. Preparation for next meeting.

 1. Identity vs. intimacy often requires more than one meeting.

Background for topical presentation. A strong sense of identity is based on self-esteem. When the young adult knows who and what she is, she is then ready for full participation in the community. She can be free to be herself because she can accept responsibility for her own actions and beliefs. She is thus ready to give or commit herself to a career, partner, or cause of her choice. Because she cares about herself and has developed a sense of self, she can care about another person. She can share her ideas and her life without fear of losing herself, or, of being dominated in the process. Mutual intimacy requires psychological readiness. The mature person is able and willing to share trust, to regulate cycles of work, recreation, procreation, and to prepare the foundation for healthy development of potential offspring.

INTIMACY VS. ISOLATION

Balancing intimacy and isolation is an ongoing task from the onset of adolescence and through young adulthood and middle age. The previous attainment of a sense of personal identity and the finding of a satisfying and productive occupation are characteristic of this period. These precipitate a new interpersonal dimension, with intimacy at one extreme and isolation at the other.

Intimacy is much more than love-making or sexual experimentation. It is the ability to love, to share with, and to care about another person without fear of losing one's self or wanting to dominate. It is based on self-knowledge and self-esteem. It implies that the young adult knows who and what he or she is, and is ready to take full responsibility for herself and her behavior. She can now participate in the community; can be self-reliant and supporting; can care about another person; can share her ideas, values, and her life with the person of her choice without fear of losing herself or of being controlled in the process. Mutual intimacy requires psychological readiness and maturity. Thus, the person is able and willing to share trust, regulate cycles of work, recreation, procreation, and prepare the foundation for the healthy development of potential offspring.

Social conditions may affect the development of intimacy, but the success or failure of this task no longer depends upon one's parents, except as they may have affected the achievement of previous stages. Intimacy does not always involve sexuality! It can include relationships between very close friends, for example, soldiers serving under dangerous conditions and circumstances and team members training and working together often develop a sense of commitment akin to intimacy.

When a sense of intimacy is not established with friends or a marriage partner, the result is a sense of isolation—of being alone without anyone to share anything with, or to care for. A sense of emptiness often follows. Complete fulfillment becomes difficult unless the individual finds a cause or an issue to which he can give of herself.

Are Your Expectations
of Your Children Realistic?

Conflict between parents and children can be classified as either "avoidable" or "unavoidable." Differences between people who are in close daily contact with each other are inevitable. However, parents who understand and use principles of human behavior in relation to the maturational and emotional age of their children can differentiate between "avoidable" and "unavoidable" confrontations of daily life.

Most "avoidable" conflicts arise from unrealistic expectations that parents and children have of each other. When parental expectations exceed the intellectual competency, understanding, and feelings of the child's capacity to perform, the results can be hurt, disappointment, and rage on both sides. Similarly, when a child expects something from his parents (for example, a promised trip, or an item which had to be postponed due to unforeseen circumstances), conflict and hurt feelings will result. Parents and children need to confront honestly why an expected behavior did not occur.

1. A situation may have been beyond the child's level of maturity or understanding, given his age, intelligence, or position. For example, it would be unrealistic to expect a sixteen-year-old to give up socializing with his group on a Saturday evening.

Likewise it would be difficult for the parents to follow through with a promise of playing a game or other activity with the child when unexpected company arrives. Such situations would be beyond the control of either parent or child and would need to be addressed at a later time.

2. Expecting "ideal" behavior in every situation is beyond most people's capacity. Children often view parents as "perfect" in the early years. It is important for parents to accept this disappointment and explain the "whys," and at the same time accept the fact that children do at times "forget" rules of good health and good manners.

3. Expecting children or teenagers to act contrary to peer norms, or in a way that would shame or embarrass them in terms of peer interaction, is unrealistic.

4. Expecting adolescents or young adults to *always* be *sensitive* to the needs and feelings of other family members is asking for something they often find difficult because of the maturational turmoil they are experiencing and the self-centeredness of young adults.

All parents hope their children will be sensitive to, and respect the feelings of, others and are appalled when their teenagers act in a totally self-centered manner. It is important to note that sensitivity develops when parents themselves are consistently respectful of their children's feelings. Many parents are unknowingly inconsiderate of their child's feelings. For example, they may constantly cut short what the child has to say; interfere with a child's game without warning; scold or berate them before company or their peers; make fun of an amusing trait or weakness; embarrass them in front of their peers; or discuss them as if they were not present. Often parents ignore or postpone promises without explanation or considering the child's feelings, and make alternative plans. Also, parents will say one thing and do another, or forget to keep a commitment and make congruent excuses. A child who has been exposed to these conditions faces adolescence with a weak sense of trust and a deep insecurity regarding his own self-worth. He is normally seeking the validation of his peers. If he lacks the respect of his parents, he tends to overemphasize his indifference to parental wishes.

When a child embarrasses us by asking an honest but inappropriate question in company parents should avoid scolding or insulting him. They should say that this is a matter to be discussed privately. This will give them an opportunity to help him understand the parents' feelings and to answer his question honestly. This will show respect for him and also for the feelings of others.

5. A peaceful home is every parent's ideal but hardly a realistic expectation. Healthy, growing children with very different personalities and ages are bound to argue, be discordant, and rivalrous. This is due to the normal innate differences between children, and their levels of emotional and social growth and cognitive understanding. All children compete for parental attention, and within limits, arguing and fighting are very healthy. Such behaviors are a source of important psychological skills, such as assertiveness. This is the ability to reach out and claim one's own; to refuse unreasonable requests and to fight constructively when necessary. It implies that we allow children to resolve issues fairly in their own way, without loss of self-esteem or feelings of revenge. Always giving in, or avoiding conflict, is not necessarily healthy. On the other hand "never being able to give in," or to recognize the rights of others, implies severe insecurity. The challenge is to teach children to give and take, to view yielding as a sign of maturity and wisdom when the other child is in the right. Learning to fight fairly and to resolve issues by searching for alternatives can be accomplished best by the examples and experiences within the family.

In addition, normal "arguing" and fighting teaches self-control and frustration tolerance. As adults we must all deal with inner and outer tensions and differences. How to think clearly and survive in the midst of differences and strife does not come about magically. This is preceded by years of childish squabbling, respecting and resolving differences fairly. This is modeled primarily upon how parents handle their own issues and those with their children. When parents refuse to fight but become stolid, withdrawn, resentful, and inwardly angry, children become confused because they have no way of dealing with their parents' exaggerated or unpredictable response to their fighting. On the other hand parents who are continuously arguing present a dismal picture of how adults cope and deal with differences. In addition, parents who "never" admit their children are right, even when they are, are teaching children that arguing and fighting is "good" only if one "wins."

Healthy parents realize that people in close proximity will eventually experience differences, and that it is human to confront them. When they can do this in a mutually respectful way, they provide their children with a positive model for resolving or settling problems in a respectful and loving manner.

6. Children should assume the same value system as their parents. Realistically it is necessary to distinguish between primary values that have their own worth and apply to all people of all ages (such as justice, honesty, love, or freedom), and secondary values that are derived from the way people interpret and live out the primary values. For example, patriotism, obedience, respect, success, work commitment, loyalty, and prestige are all secondary values which when carried to an extreme can be corrosive to family relationships. One can be totally committed to his work because he loves his family, but if he becomes a workaholic he is likely to hurt himself as well as the very people he is providing for. Secondary values are virtuous up to a point because they relate to the culture of our time. For example, until recently women could not enter professions reserved for men, such as engineering or mechanics. Today such a value system would be considered sexist, and women are free to enter any occupation of their choice.

Therefore, if parents fail to distinguish between the primary and secondary values, conflict can result. They need to be aware of social changes in attitudes and behavior and recognize that the world of their children is somewhat different from the world in which they grew up. It is much more important that they understand and assist their children to select the appropriate secondary values that can help them to incorporate the primary values. Much friction can ensue when parents insist that children dress a certain way, practice the same religion, go to prestigious colleges (for which they are not ready), earn money and prestige in certain ways, or even love only certain people—all under the guise that it is for their own good! It would be infinitely more productive if parents encouraged honesty and self-awareness; helped them work up to their potential; helped them decide on a career that meets their needs; or let them discover their beliefs and love in their own way. This type of self-fulfillment would be a great affirmation of effective and loving parenting and would enable the child to lead a successful life.

Effective parenting does not mean perfection, but rather the ability to use mistakes honestly and in a constructive manner. Parental authority is not compromised when parents can admit to an error, acknowledge feelings, and avoid hasty judgments. An apology or admission of error actually can encourage the child to participate in the resolution of a problem. Thus, the child learns firsthand that we can use our mistakes constructively.

Some admonishments:

1. Children do not need parents as friends. They need parents who love and respect them enough to control and set limits for them.

2. Children need to know their parents believe in their primary values strongly enough to uphold them and not allow manipulation. This provides them with credibility and a sense of security.

3. Parents who fear saying "no" to destructive behavior are discouraging frustration tolerance. Children need to learn how to handle frustration. Giving in to their every wish denies them the sensitivity of guidelines and the ability to judge their own behavior and that of others.

4. Parents need to respond to negative acting out by understanding the feelings that provoked the behavior and by helping the child to learn there are alternative ways of making an impression than "getting his way."

5. Parents need to make clear that negative behavior results in negative consequences.

Otherwise parental authority will be compromised and the child cannot develop a sense of control over his own life. It is common in anxious, insecure children to keep testing limits. Therefore, when parents fail to set limits, his security is being threatened.

Parents need to realize that even bright and intellectually precocious children are still children who are limited in experience and psychoemotional development. They need affection, encouragement, and support along with the limits and discipline that loving parents can provide in order for them to be able to handle the problems and opportunities of young adulthood.

Good Study Tips

The basic premises of good study habits are self-discipline; high motivation, and being achievement-oriented.

Schedule

1. Set a daily schedule.

2. Allow no interference—stick to it.

3. Take advantage of your natural inclinations: if you are a day-lily, do your studying as early as possible. If you are a night-owl, select a later time for studying.

4. Approach the more difficult subjects first. Give secondary place to easier subjects.

5. Post your schedule, and after experimentation, stick to it without fail. Do other tasks (for example, laundry and shopping) during your free time.

6. Allow yourself some relaxation time.

Place

1. Choose a small, well-lighted, ventilated, and uncluttered place.

2. Use a cleared table-top and straight-backed chair.

3. Have pencils, pens, paper pads, 3″ × 5″ cards, and typewriter handy.

4. Keep handy any reference books you may need, for example, a dictionary or encyclopedia.

5. Get up and stretch or walk around periodically to improve circulation.

6. Avoid TV, radio, ticking clocks, novels, phones, unanswered letters, or other distractions. Do not study in an easy chair or in bed. These are for reading, not studying!

Mental Attitude

1. Begin work immediately. Efficient use of time results in a sense of accomplishment.

2. Concentrate on your task—concentration demands 100-percent attention!

3. Look for logical relationships between sentences, paragraphs, and sections of textbooks or reference works.

4. Absorb yourself in your study so that it becomes pleasurable and satisfying.

5. Leave your desk with the good feeling of having achieved what you had planned or were assigned to do, even if this involves memorization or repetition.

Helpful Procedures

1. Use some of the following ideas to master a book.

   ● Use 3" × 5" cards. Place the date on the card, and indicate the author's full name; title of book; publisher's name and location; and the year of publication.

   ● If the book is from a library, indicate the call number and library name on the card, too.

   ● Adopt the *PQRST* procedure.

2. *P—Preread* the book's preface or foreword to determine its purpose and scope. Review the table of contents to get an overview.

   ● Establish bridges between what you know and what the book offers, and between the chapters of the book.

   ● Size up the structure of the material and its logical development.

   ● Skim the beginning paragraphs of each chapter to familiarize youself with the author's approach, style, and point of view.

3. *Q—Question* yourself.

   ● How much do you know about the subject?

   ● To which parts should you give the most attention?

   ● Which part is more important or critical?

4. *R—Read* carefully.

   ● Make notes of any items you want to recall or use. List page numbers, names, statistics, details, or style. List whatever you think you might need later on.

   ● Read against time—try to cover more pages each day. You will understand more as you read more.

   ● Grasp concepts, and use analogies. Note nouns, verbs and important modifiers.

   ● Learn to distinguish thesis statements (that make a point) from corroborative statements (that confirm a point).

   ● Expository, explanatory paragraphs use topic sentences, supporting sentences, and clinching sentences. Each sentence that follows a topic sentence narrows down the subject, widens your knowledge, and verifies the topic sentence.

   ● Know about different methods of constructing paragraphs (such as expository, descriptive or narrative). This will help you zero in on the essential elements of your reading.

- To speed up your reading, widen your view. Decrease the number of fixations your eyes must make per line. Decrease your fatigue; grasp more meaning by concentrating on groups of words. Push yourself to a speed that is initially uncomfortable, and keep pressing yourself. Strive to get the meaning.

5. *S—Summarize.*
    - Write a résumé of each chapter or other book division. Use the logical connection of ideas.
    - Reconstruct material to fix it in your mind.

6. *T—Think.*
    - Think about what you have learned.
    - Test youself: Do you agree with the author, or disagree? Write out your arguments and support them.
    - Develop critical acumen.

Vocabulary Building

1. Write down new words on 3″ × 5″ cards.
2. Look up meanings, and record derivations.
3. Record multiple meanings and read them in context.
4. Alphabetize cards, and keep them handy in a box.
5. Review and use these words in conversation and in writing.

Memorization

1. If you are a visual learner, repeated reading of a paragraph will help fix it in your mind.
2. If you are an oral learner, record the material and listen to it often.
3. A combination of these two methods works for most people.
4. Mnemonic devices are also effective. Relating a concept to a familiar place or subject is helpful. Memorization is *mastery;* successful study is *dominion;* the feeling of accomplishment is your *reward.*

Reading a Novel

1. Note the title and author on a 3″ × 5″ card.
2. Find the theme, central idea, or message.
3. What is the tone of the book: serious? whimsical? tragic? humorous?
4. Sketch out the structural characteristics: note logic, chronology, unusual or extraordinary features, and the direction of the narrative.
5. Note the situation or story line, and level of suspense.
6. What is the setting? What period or place in history? What sort of character development takes place? What is the tone?
7. What is the style (diction or symbols)?

HELPING CHILDREN
MAKE CAREER PLANS

Career decision making is an ongoing process, not an event that occurs at a given time. Your child's future career will be influenced by events that occur beginning in the preschool years and continue through all of adult life. Here are some ways in which you can aid your child in positive career development.

- Encourage your child to ask and think about the question, "What will I be when I grow up?" In the early years, children's hopes are often expressed in fantasy terms, especially during play. You will hear things such as, "I'm Daddy and I'm Superman, and you're Mommy and you're Wonder Woman." Do not criticize such statements. Your child is exploring who he or she is and the kind of person he is becoming. It will help you to understand him or her better if you let your child talk in this way. Provide toys that encourage experimentation through play with many different jobs.

- Do not discourage your child from planning particular careers at an early age. It is better to ask, "Why does this appeal to you?" than it is to say something like "You wouldn't like to do that" or "That's a terrible job" or "That's completely unrealistic." Until major action decisions have to be made, it is better to let your child think about a wide range of possible job choices.

- Try to help your child think about alternative choices. A good question to ask is, "If for some reason you couldn't do this, what other thing would you want to do?" It will help you learn more about your child, and it will help her or him to broaden the basis for career decision making. Talking about your own alternate career choices will also help in this. For example, discuss jobs you have had in the past, or changes you might be considering in your present occupation.

- Try to eliminate sex bias in thinking about your child's future career. Your daughter may very well wish to enter an occupation you now think of as "masculine," or your son might want to enter one that you consider "feminine." Do not discourage them from thinking about such occupations. Times are changing, and they will need extra measures of your emotional support. If the child next door discourages your daughter from being a doctor because "girls are nurses," arrange for your daughter to speak to a woman doctor if you can. If you cannot, point out women who are in traditionally male jobs. Emphasize that a person's sex does not really matter, it's ability that counts.

- Do not hesitate to respond when your child asks, "What do you think I should be when I grow up?" Try to make it clear that it is more important that he or she be happy than become what you would like. However, you can point out particular talents that he or she possesses and discuss the jobs that would utilize these traits.

- Tell your child about the work you do. Try to do so in a positive way so that your child will gain respect for you by respecting what you do. Neither encourage nor discourage your child from considering your occupation. The important thing is that your child sees that you, through your work, are making contributions to society.

- Encourage your child to ask people about their jobs. Make use of your friends who are in the occupations your child is considering. Emphasize the seeking of information, not firm advice, from such persons. If your child is particularly interested, ask a friend if he or she can visit to see what the job actually involves.

- Take your child on field trips to see various people at work in factories, offices, auto mechanic shops, and so forth. This is very helpful in letting children acquire a realistic view of a variety of jobs.

- Help your child explore hobbies and other leisure-time activities that are productive and useful. Sometimes such activities can lead to career choices. Whether they do or not is unimportant. What is important is that they can help your child see himself or herself as one who can accomplish something successfully.

- Help your child understand how very important her or his schoolwork will be in later job decisions. Show them how such subjects as reading, arithmetic, and communications are used in almost all occupations. In short, help them understand that what they are learning in school has relevance in real life.

- Encourage your child to engage in part-time work outside the home. If such work is done for pay, you can talk to your child about basic elements in the free enterprise system. Whether or not the work is for pay, it can be valuable in two ways: (1) it can help your child explore career interests and (2) it can help your child discover the sense of accomplishment and self-pride that can come from work. It also teaches organization and a sense of responsibility.

- Encourage your child to discuss with teachers and counselors, career plans, and hopes. After such visits, talk with your children about what they learned. Feel free to tell them what you think. In doing so make it clear that you are expressing your opinion, not telling them what to do with their lives. Do not refuse to discuss such matters with your children just because you do not know the answers.

- Visit the schools your children attend. If your child has been discussing career plans with a teacher or counselor at school, seek that person out and ask such questions as, "Do you think this career is suitable in view of my child's strengths and weaknesses?"; "What are the best schools for pursuing this field of study?"; "What is the employment outlook for this career?" You will often learn much and you will certainly help techers and counselors to help your children more if you are willing to talk to them.

- Help your child understand that it will be equally important to acquire a set of specific job skills *and* a set of adaptable skills for occupational success. For example, if your child is considering a career in journalism, it would be wise to have a broad base of academic subjects that might be used in other fields besides journalism. Help him understand that many occupations are interrelated.

- Remember a college degree is no longer the best or surest route to occupational success. If your child is in high school, encourage him or her to think about all kinds of postsecondary educational opportunities. Try to help your child think about a variety or *kinds* of postsecondary educational opportunities, for example: all-volunteer armed forces; vocational schools; or community colleges. Emphasize the wide choice that exists, and that no choice needs to be final because each choice can lead to another, either in the same field or a different one.

Your child's career choices will certainly affect your *future as well as your child's. In this sense, you have a* right, *as well as a responsibility, to be active in helping your child make career plans.*

U.S. Department of Health, Education and Welfare Office of Education.

SEXUALITY AND YOUR TEENAGER

Recent studies indicate that the average age at which teenagers engage in sexual intercourse appears to be sixteen. At least two-thirds of all teenagers have had a sexual experience by age nineteen. Parents, schools, churches, and synagogues all maintain a "hands-off" policy in terms of early sexual exploration, but recent figures indicate that at least 11 million kids reportedly have had sexual relations. By 1981 the number rose to 13 million, with 1.3 million girls becoming pregnant. This means that one out of every five babies is born to a teenage mother. This surely is not what most parents want for their children, yet cultural forces seem to contradict the prohibitions of home, school, and religious institutions.

The media use sex to sell everything from cars to clothes; cigarettes to detergents, and even dog food. TV shows, movies, magazines, books, and popular music all glamorize sexuality to the point that few teenagers can resist the constant bombardment. Physical forces within the teenager's body plus cultural stimuli seem to be stronger and more immediate than the forces against sex. Because no parent can be sure that his child will be unaffected, it is important that they help their teenagers to deal with the complex world of junior high and high school. Children need guidance in knowing how to take charge of and channel their complex feelings, their impulses, and their lives. Even more important, parents need to start as early as possible to provide them with certain guidelines.

1. Be sure that clear limits are set regarding *where* they can go, *when* they go, with whom, and when they can be expected to return. These rules should be reasonable and flexible in accordance with their age and ability to accept responsibility.

2. Help them to accept responsibility for themselves and their behavior—and clearly state the consequences for noncompliance.

3. Demonstrate your affection for your children and your mate openly and freely.

4. Explain the facts about sex honestly and forthrightly. If your feel embarrased, say so, and give them books about it that are appropriate to their age and experience. Never make them feel ashamed of themselves as sexual beings.

5. Be understanding of the outside peer pressure, particlarly in reference to sexual experience. Help them understand the responsibility and consequences attendant to their actions.

Most families raise their children according to certain rules. The more consistently these rules are enforced during early childhood, the easier it will be when children reach puberty. However, some parents tend to worry that their children will be unduly influenced by peer pressure and become rule-bound—which may boomerang. In general children of twelve to thirteen should not be allowed to "hang out" or go on "single dates." However, they should be encouraged to socialize in accordance to rules specified by their parents—that is, what kind of party they can attend or give; kinds of supervision; transportation to and from; and curfew. All these should be negotiated before the event. The child needs to know that these rules are subject to modification as he matures.

When parents are willing to listen and take the time to discuss these matters, their children will trust their judgment and accept guidelines as evidence of parental love and caring. This system works well when parents in a neighborhood or school can all agree on a "dating age," transportation, curfews, supervision, and kinds of parties their children can have or attend. Thus, when all their friends have similar limits, the pressure will decrease on both parents and children. However, if such cooperation is not available, parents need to uphold their own rules in a fair firm but reasonable fashion. Succumbing to "everybody else is going" or "doing it" is unwise and leads to manipulation by children.

Teenagers cannot learn to be reliable and make intelligent choices without experience. Parents must start as soon as possible to provide opportunities for them to become responsible. Though sexual decision making is not part of early childhood training, learning to make decisions and being responsible for the consequences should start early. For example, parents should allow children to choose the clothes they wear each day; to perform certain chores; to be responsible for the care of their teeth, hair, body hygiene; and to choose activities that involve decision-making and responsibility. This improves their sense of autonomy and helps them to realize that decisions also have consequences. If they make errors, they can learn from them, and are apt to be more discerning. This type of training prepares them to make intelligent choices, use their initiative, and develop impulse control and self-respect. This type of child usually is not easily led by others, or forced into doing something simply to impress others.

Despite the furor over the "world needing love" most people find the spontaneous and open show of affection quite difficult. Consequently, while sex is constantly talked about or inferred in various ways, it remains something secretive and mysterious. This is not to say that parents should act out sexually, but kissing and hugging your children and your mate results in good feelings and a healthy attitude. It helps children to realize that mature love can be wonderful between people who respect and love each other and are not afraid to be close and intimate. Thus parental attitudes and behavior can greatly influence children's sexual behavior and what they will expect from their own partner.

Sex education should be the responsibility of the parents. However, many parents are puzzled as to when, how, and how much they should teach their children. Others feel unable to approach the subject without embarrassment. Parents should avoid the "birds and the bees" explanation or stalling with "wait until you're older." If parent–child communication is comfortable, children usually approach their parents with questions as they are ready. Parents should take the time to find out what the child already knows and then respond as honestly as possible. Answers that are too involved are confusing, and simplistic answers tend to be trite and evasive. This is an opportunity for parents and children to become closer and establish respect for each other's personhood. Giving them the idea that sex is "dirty" or "nothing to talk about" will distort the child's idea of the role of sex in adult life. It also forces him to seek answers from outsiders who may not have his welfare in mind. Most of all the parent loses his opportunity to teach his child how to decide what is appropriate for him. Without facts he cannot make wise decisions. Honest discussion between parents and children about this important subject helps strengthen the bond between them.

The teenager is subject to several types of pressure at this time of life. His rapidly changing body exerts considerable pressure as his reproductive system matures. He experiences new feelings and sensations, and disturbing thoughts tend to preoccupy him.

This is normal, natural, and involuntary. He is not "bad" or thinking "dirty thoughts." How to respond to these feelings becomes a central issue. Therefore, learning about sexual behavior and how to control it becomes a critical problem. In addition the adolescent is now beginning to establish a sense of personal identity that causes him to assert his independence from parents. These intense and somewhat fearful emotional issues are experienced by both sexes.

An early expression of sexual feelings is masturbation. Originally prohibited by some religions, it is currently medically approved as a normal outlet for sexual desire when intercourse is not appropriate. It has no ill effects whatsoever, unless parents or other adults impose shame and guilt, or unless it becomes an obsession. If understood and ignored it will not interfere with normal sexual activity and tends to prevent sexual acting out.

Sexual information should also include various deviations such as homosexuality and the danger of venereal diseases and AIDS. Many excellent pamphlets and books are available on these subjects. A talk with the family physician would be an excellent source of information. Both girls and boys should be informed on the dangers inherent in teenage pregnancy or abortion. Birth control methods should be openly discussed and be made available as necessary to both sexes.

Peer pressure is a constant problem at this period and cannot be eliminated. The pressure to date, to be popular, or to be approved by one's group cannot be denied. Not being popular with one's group is akin to being a social failure! Girls in particular are especially vulnerable to sexual advances and plays. The "You would if you loved me" approach should be explained as a very self-serving and irresponsible request. Sex is no proof of love, and love is much more than sex. Youths need to be reassured of the facts, and be helped to realize that the consequences of irresponsible sex are long lasting, and devastating to themselves, as well as to the baby that might well be the result of uncontrolled and insistent feelings (rather than of real and lasting affection). Maturity is an individual matter and occurs at a different rate with different people. Slow maturation often incites put-downs and "wise cracks" that are hard to withstand. However, those who develop the necessary self-confidence that enables them to mature at their own pace usually become move loving, patient, and interesting young adults who attract many friends and lead far more interesting lives.

Adolescents who come home to empty homes find it difficult to withstand the combined pressure from precocious and insistent boyfriends or girlfriends and their own curosity and desire. Parents who must work should encourage their young adult children to participate in some activity, sports, or part-time work that will occupy the teenager in a constructive way. If this is not possible they must be sure the child has specific duties and/or responsibilities as well as some kind of reward or recognition. The young adolescent resents supervision, but if these tasks are assigned in terms of "I need your help." or "You were so good at . . ." or "Would you help me to prepare this." or "Could you do that when you get home?" These attitudes make the child feel valuable, respected, and trusted.

In addition to all this parents need to monitor TV, radio, and the media. Though the distorted image of sexual activity on TV cannot be totally avoided it can be counterbalanced by discussing these programs with children and getting their opinions on them.

In summary, teenagers are subject to enormous pressures for sexual exploration from within and without. They need to be protected from the media blitz, from intense peer pressure, and from lack of honest information. Parents who assist them to place sex in a wholesome context as part, but not all, of a person's appeal will be helping them to survive this enormous and constant pressure. Their respect, love, and concern for their teenager's emerging sexuality and developing identity will help their teenager to handle intimacy with integrity.

Final Suggestions

1. Engage them in discussion rather than moralizing about responsible attitudes toward sex.

2. Some pertinent questions a parent can suggest the teenager ask himself are:

   a. Am I ready to engage in sexual activity?

   b. Is my partner ready?

   c. Are *we* ready?

   d. Are we really in love?

   e. Is love important to sex?

   f. Do I want to have sex with just anyone?

   g. Does everyone do it?

   h. Is that a good reason for me to do it?

   i. Can I handle the consequences?

   j. What are the advantages or disadvantages of waiting or of putting it off? Does it make any sense?

AT HOME WITH YOUR TEENAGER

Living with today's teenager is like being on a roller coaster. The unpredictability of wide mood swings is a source of puzzlement and distress to the entire family. Obedience has changed to rebellion or defiance; agreement, to dissension or ridicule; long-standing practices and rules are suddenly senseless or ignored; formerly effective disciplinary actions become useless or unenforceable! Along with behavioral characteristics, the striking physical, emotional, and social changes that accompany adolescence inevitably cause upheaval and disruption in most families. Slowly, parents realize and accept the need to alter their usual way of thinking and reacting to their teenager. Where tender loving care previously produced positive results, it seems that something "more" or different is needed to assist the teenager in this quest for maturity.

That "more" is not any technical skill, but learning how to express certain crucial qualities that will help the adolescent to at least remain on talking terms with his parents. Adolescents seem to require more *listening to;* a *greater tolerance* for the unpredictable and abrupt daily changes of mood, attitude, and behavior; and a *willingness to trust them more.*

Parents need to understand that like that of little children, the average teenager's concept of time is endless. Whereas parents are harried and pushed by endless cares and responsibilities, the teenager seems to be wasting an inordinate amount of time—daydreaming! Developmentally this "time" really has significant psychological purposes. Through fantasy, he tries out various roles related to his search for the direction his adult life will eventually take. Daydreams can actually increase his motivation to achieve and are often the principal factors in selecting a career. Fantasy also helps him to picture himself in various roles: head of a research lab; a famous actor; a successful athlete; or a powerful business executive. Repetitive daydreams are powerful instigators of later decisions, and attest to his powers of obsevation. They are used to practice reaction to future situations that worry him—like interviews, getting a new job, a new girlfriend, or joining a team. Some fantasies act as safety valves to escape or reduce tension. He might be resolving a fear-producing or stressful situation, or reliving an embarrassing encounter to which he may be trying alternative solutions. Thus, what often appears to be a gross waste of time to an adult actually functions as a vital problem-solving experience to the teenager.

Another mysterious and annoying teenage practice is the pointless and seemingly endless conversations between teenagers. The phone is in constant use, often at the cost of homework completion. And yet, these long, rambling, and irritating discussions are the chief source whereby youngsters check out their perceptions of the world around them and gain a more realistic view of themselves and of others. This is known as consensual validation (or being considered an "OK boy or girl") and is the principal way by which teenagers share opinions, reactions, and perceptions in a safe and nonthreatening atmosphere.

Legitimately, most parents are concerned that their teenager comply with the work ethic of our society, realizing that achievement of any goal requires good work habits, motivation, initiative, and training. Thus, the question of holding a part-time job while going to school can present problems. When teenagers have a job, some parents feel this develops a healthy attitude toward work, helps the youngster to organize himself, and teaches him about money. Others feel their teenager should concentrate on excelling in academics and school activities. Generally, many adolescents are eager to hold part-time jobs due to the considerable financial outlay required by their activities, as well as the pleasure and self-esteem provided by their weekly paycheck. A job that does not interfere with the teenager's schoolwork can have numerous benefits. It can teach the teenager about the adult world; use and value of money; responsibility; learning to take directions; and self-confidence. Parents should clearly express their expectations regarding this matter, but allow the child to make his choice.

The average teenager is acutely sensitive to criticism and put-downs. Most of them can deal with constructive criticism when it is honest and offset by their good points. However, disparaging comparisons that implicitly carry a message of inferiority or failure should be avoided. Most adolescents are painfully aware of their weaknesses and their standing, and are able to identify the talent and abilities of their group. Though parents may feel that "sooner or later" they have to know how they stack up in the "real world," parents need to realize that the competitive nature of the teenager provides him with adequate feedback about his own worth. Therefore, in view of the constant inner turmoil the teenager experiences about his own adequacy, parents should remember that he needs to feel he is "tops" with them. This feeling helps him to be more realistic about what he can do about any of his inadequacies.

Another futile parental practice is comparing him to "what you did" or "could do" at his age. The world is constantly changing, to say nothing of the fact that you and your teenager are certainly not alike, and are living in different ages. In reality "when I was your age I" is basically a form of venting anger towards a youngster who has had little to say about the world around him. The message he receives is one of personal inadequacy and he will respond with defensive anger and resistance, while inwardly feeling fearful and insecure.

When parents are concerned about the teenager's failure to concentrate and apply himself to his schoolwork, it is better to express these concerns frankly and openly with him. He will respond with understanding to legitimate concerns about a situation which, in all probability, is indicative of his own inner fear of inadequacy. Parents should help him express his feelings and help him seek out some alternatives. He can do this better when he feels love and support rather than contempt and rejection. Remember, he too is disappointed and fearful of his own perceived inadequacy.

The aim of adolescence is ultimately to be independent of parents—and certainly most parents wish to accomplish that same goal. Yet in many ways teenagers lack the knowledge and experience to deal with the many problems arising at this age. Thus, parents are faced with resolving problems that arise from poor decisions made by their teenager's lack of experience. If he has made a poor decision or choice, responsibility for that decision must be his. Unwise use of money, choice of clothing, hair style, where and when they go out and their time of return are all issues that can be sources of difficulty. Parents need not be passive—they need to discuss these issues openly, set clear limits as well as the consequences of noncompliance. Once the limits are set, parents need to remain interested and share their opinions. When the teenager makes errors in judgment or goes beyond the limits, calmly enforce the consequences, and try to discuss how future errors can be avoided. The more active a role the parent plays as a consultant the better decisions the teenager can make.

Issues such as school courses or activities, colleges they should apply to, parties they should attend or give, friends they make, smoking or drinking, and after-school jobs are all typical adolescent concerns. The adolescent wants parental views, but his approach in soliciting this can often be misleading. When your sixteen-year-old informs you she is about to "take a weekend job as a cocktail waitress" because "the money is good," it is very tempting to forbid this in no uncertain terms. Yet, the fact that she shares this with you indicates that she is really seeking your advice. Saying "no" or giving a "but" answer does not help her understand your views and often causes withdrawal. However, spending a little time discussing it with her—giving your opinion and having her look at consequences and other options—will go far in getting her to see the incongruence of such a move. It helps her to realize that you consider her a reasonable person and that you love her enough to reason things out with her.

Problems of drinking and driving, of sex and drugs are very prevalent and worrisome to parents. However, parental advice and viewpoints are not resisted as much as parents might think. Unfortunately, emotional overtones are so strong that parents have a hard time dealing with these. We must remember that adolescents want parental guidelines and reactions on these issues more than ever. They welcome confirmation that their parents do care and love them enough to say, "Oh I know you're older now—and I can't really stop you, but at least hear me out, and understand why I don't like to see you do these things and how important you are to me!" One father even obtained a filmstrip from a driver-education class to convince his teenage son of the dangers of drinking and driving. Another mother gave up smoking to show her daughter how much she cared for her, and improved her communication pattern to facilitate a more positive relationship.

As adolescents assume decision-making responsibilities for their lives, parents should permit their relationship to grow into one between mutually concerned but independent adults. This helps the adolescent to respect and value himself because his parents recognize and respect him as a young self-reliant adult. Adolescents grow at individual rates and therefore it is difficult to state at exactly which point they are ready to assume independent responsibility, but this is a gradual process and parents need to take their cues from their own children. If it has been a family practice to help the child assume those responsibilities for which he is ready as he grows from one stage to another, then parents will know *when* and *when not* to let go.

The typical psychological instability and restlessness of children growing into young adults can make limit setting a difficult issue. Yet, given this instability, the need for a stable, well-structured, predictable, external world is as great at this stage of development as it was when they were infants! Parents need to set fair, firm, consistent limits and clear expectations for their adolescents. This will relieve some of the stress and provide the security of an external structure needed by adolescents. The kind of rules and expectations comfortable for one family may differ from those of another. The emphasis is on *working out* the rules together—between parents and adolescents—so that each knows what he can expect from the other. Inconsistency can prove disastrous. Just as teenagers need to understand the limits set upon them, they also should be made aware of their privileges. Privileges and responsibility go together and should be in balance. The adolescent with too many responsibilities feels frustrated, overburdened, and inadequate. The adolescent with too many privileges acquires an unrealistic view of life and becomes anxious and bored.

Appreciation of the teenagers' special talents and abilities is very often overlooked. Even though we are in an age of specialization, it appears that teenagers are expected to be generalists. For example, grade point averages commonly show the students' performance across the board. Grades in various subjects are lumped together, thus not giving recognition to the areas of strength. This often leads to discouragement. Though it is unwise to disregard society's demand for a certain level of general achievement, this demand can be tempered by recognition of the child's individual talent. Parents need to distinguish beween talent and achievement. Discovery of talent inevitably requires many trials and errors. Therefore, children should be encouraged to participate and experience a wide variety of activities. Early achievement in any subject or activity does not necessarily imply talent. But, through these encounters of failures, disappointments, success, awards, frustrations, and defeats, the adolescent develops a healthy personality and becomes more realistic about his own potential. Parents must look beyond school grades and praise other attributes their children surely have. It is not the talents parents want, but rather the talent the youngster himself actually has and develops that will make the difference in his life—and that is what should be acknowledged by the parents.

At best, adolescence is a time of transition and of rapid changes and experimentations because the maturation process is not easy or smooth. If problems can be confronted honestly and trustingly by both parents and adolescents, a suitable resolution can be found. Parents should be specific, practical, and forthright. They should encourage and respect the growth, independence, and ability of their children. Learn to share your ideals, goals, and values with your child. There is no magic formula that guarantees parental success in this difficult relationship, but keeping these principles in mind will assist you to help them become successful, happy, and effective adults.

Based on "How to Live Almost Happily with a Teenager," by Drs. Joel and Lois Davits, McCall's Magazine, *January 1981.*

Meetings 8, 9, 10
A Review

A. Greetings and opening remarks.
1. Participants check attendance sheet.
2. Leader reviews first five stages of development.
3. Leader encourages questions and comments as well as the sharing of experiences of the past week.
4. Leader helps parents to use new concepts and information to analyze interaction between themselves and their children and to test out alternative responses.
B. Topical presentation: Human relations training and communication skills.
C. Human relations training exercises.
1. Positive and negative feelings.
   a. Parents are asked to list as many "positive feeling" remarks as they can think of in a one-minute interval.
   b. Leader asks "How many listed twelve or more? ten or more? eight or more?"
   c. Leader has respondents read these to the group.
   d. Parents are asked to list as many "negative feeling" remarks as they can think of in a one-minute interval.
   e. Leader again asks how many words were listed.
   f. Leader asks respondents to share these remarks with the group.
   g. Usually more negative than positive feeling-words are listed!
2. Labeling feelings.
   a. Leader distributes typed sample statements adapted from previous groups (see appendix A). Each parent is to read the statements and identify and label the primary feelings expressed or implied.
   b. Leader will read other statements for additional practice or labeling feelings until parents are able to do this easily and accurately.
3. Classifying responses (additive, subtractive, and interchangeable).
   a. Leader presents statements that have two or three responses. Parents are to classify responses as additive, subtractive, or interchangeable.
   b. Leader continues this exercise until parents feel comfortable and can respond accurately and easily.
D. Discussion highlights.
1. Parents base discussion on above exercises as they apply to interactions with their own children.

E.   Preparation for next meeting.
    1.   Each parent is requested to write up or bring in at least one interpersonal encounter with his or her child to use in role-playing to implement the above training.
    2.   Refer to human relations training, communication, and problem solving skills in appendix A.

Background for topical presentation: The suggested presentation is based on the manual entitled *Human Relations Training* by Sydnor, Akridge, and Parkhill. The purpose of human relations training is to improve the effectiveness of our interaction with one another and to enhance personal and interpersonal growth. Communication, a basic form of interaction with others, is based on empathic understanding of what others are saying to us. That is, the message is not just the words, but the feeling with which the words are said. In responding to others it is important to recognize and accurately label these feelings.

Attending behaviors (such as eye contact, concentration on what the person is trying to communicate, and empathy and respect for the speaker) are all basic to communication skills. Responses generally fall into five categories:

1.   *Interchangeable.* Respondent picks up meaning of statement and places it in the same feeling dimension.
2.   *Subtractive.* Respondent bypasses meaning and feeling and responds with a peripheral remark.
3.   *Additive.* Respondent picks up meaning and labels feelings at a deeper level.
4.   *Confrontative.* Respondent points out expressed or implied discrepancies in what has been said, or between words and actions.
5.   *Summary Feelings Statement.* Respondent unifies content of the expressed experiential theme with the feelings expressed or implied.

Usually, interchangeable and additive responses assist the clarification process, which helps the person to feel better understood about what he is experiencing.

Meetings 11, 12, and 13
A Review

A. Greetings and opening remarks.
    1. Check attendance.
    2. Leader encourages examination of problems and analysis of solutions that have failed.
B. Human relations training—communication skills.
    1. Leader continues exercises in identification of feelings for review.
    2. Feelings continue to be labeled.
    3. Response to content and feelings (additive, subtractive, interchangeable, confrontative, or summary feelings statement).
    4. Sample exercise (see appendix for sample statements).
        a. Group is paired off; pairs make statements to each other and the helper's response is labeled by his or her partner. Each one labels the other partner's response.
        b. Group decides whether helper responded and labeled feeling accurately and whether response was additive, subtractive, interchangeable, and so on.
        c. Parents continue to present personal interactions with their children; role-playing continues.
C. Topical presentation: Problem-solving skills.
    1. Listen to what the child is saying.
    2. Identify and label his feelings.
    3. Respond to feelings empathically.
    4. Ask the child what he can do about the situation.
    5. Help the child explore alternatives.
    6. Praise the child's efforts to find own solution.
    7. Do not give ready-made solutions. You may give suggestions or opinions, but the only solution worthwhile is that which the child can implement on his own.

    Sample Interaction between Mother and Child.
    Child: (Very agitated) I'd like to punch that Jimmy! He's such a jerk. He's always picking on me—punching me and everything!
    Mother: O, I'm sorry—you must feel pretty angry about that!

Child: I hate him, I hate him—he's a bully. I'd like to punch his face in. If only he wasn't bigger than me!

Mother: Yeah, I certainly can understand how you'd like to sock him back—but you're worrying because he's bigger than you.

Child: Yeah, he fights dirty, too. He's a real bully.

Mother: You're really mad because he doesn't fight fair. Isn't there some way—some other way of handling this? What do you think?

Child: I don't know. I'd like to kill him. He picks on kids when nobody is around.

Mother: You mean when you're alone he'll start a fight? Is there anyone you could walk home with?

Child: Yeah, there's David and Paul, but they go to soccer practice four times a week. Gee, maybe I could join them and stay for—or maybe I could come home the back way—

D.   Using problem-solving skills.
    1.   Leader requests parents to react to sample interactions as in the above example.
    2.   Leader intensifies action-oriented strategies, and role-playing.

    Examples:

    I wonder why you usually interrupt Mary and not Jean?

    You seem to be turning requests into orders—have you thought how your child feels when you do this?

    Is that really what you want—being a martyr to your family?

    You seem to find it hard to finish a sentence.

    I wonder why you leave things open-ended—how does that affect the children?

E.   Preparation for termination.
    1.   Parents continue to bring sample behaviors and interactions for role-playing.

Meeting 14
A Review

A. Greetings and opening remarks.
   1. Check attendance.
   2. Review; questions; and comments.
   3. Allay fears and anxiety of reality testing.
   4. Deepen parent's feelings of competence, confidence, and self-worth.
B. Human relations training: Communication and problem-solving skills.
   1. Practice exercises continue—group interacts freely.
   2. Role-playing has become very productive—parents take turns being "child" or "parent."
   3. Leader should intersperse an analysis of some situations.
   4. Leader is careful to use recommended approaches.
   5. Leader's role is supportive—parents do most of the guiding at this point.
C. Suggested lead statements.
   1. Leads in searching for alternatives.
      a. "Because you resent your in-laws so bitterly and you always get migraines when they visit, what other way could your family celebrate birthdays?"
      b. "Maybe we should look at what's really happening now, and then consider what you really want to have happen."
      c. "OK, now you've gotten your family to listen—how can you get them to cooperate?"
   2. Leads in confronting rationalizations.
      a. "OK, you've given us all the 'head' reasons—now can you identify your real feelings?"
      b. "You seem to know exactly what can be done—but you don't seem to deal with how you feel about doing it!"
      c. "Those are all good reasons for not getting at it, but you seem to be saying that you're really scared of the enormous responsibility."
      d. "We seem to come up with the same reasons over and over—can you see the connection between these and your fear of being alone?"
D. Preparation for termination.
      a. Hand out parent bibliography.

Meeting 15
Final Meeting: A Review

A. Greetings and opening remarks.
   1. Allay fears and anxiety about impending separation.
   2. Express regret, but also your trust of their innate ability for continued growth.
   3. Encourage parents to exchange phone numbers and make arrangements to continue relationship with one another.
B. Suggested lead statements.
   1. Leads to prepare for termination.
      a. "I wonder what you see ahead for you and your family?"
      b. "How can you use the experience we've had together?"
      c. "Where do you think you can go from here?"
      d. "How can we handle these feelings if they should reoccur?"
      e. "What can we reasonably expect from _____ ?"
      f. "What can we do when things get ahead of us?"
      g. "Suppose you find yourself slipping back to old ways—what can you do about it?"
C. Note progress.
   1. Leader requests parents complete second sentence completion survey.
   2. Leader praises parents on their progress after they compare the answers from the first survey with their present answers.
   3. Leader recognizes their sense of competence and self-esteem.
   4. Leader thanks the group for their cooperation, and asks them to complete the evaluation of their group experience, which should appear at the bottom of their initial registration form.
   5. Leader collects sheets and bids group farewell.

Appendix A
Organizational Materials
and Supplementary Handouts

SENTENCE COMPLETION SURVEY

1. My children please me most when _____ .

2. I think growing up is _____ .

3. I am determined _____ .

4. I am happiest when _____ .

5. The worst thing my children can do is _____ .

6. When things go wrong I _____ .

7. I do not like to be _____ .

8. Spouses _____ .

9. I like it best when _____ .

10. The most important thing to me _____ .

11. At home we _____ .

12. I think that life is _____ .

13. I try _____ .

14. Children should _____ .

15. I want to know _____ .

16. It is impossible _____ .

17. If only _____ .

18. I can't do what I want because _____ .

19. What keeps me going _____ .

20. To me people _____ .

21. All my life _____ .

22. My family _____ .

23. Sometimes my feelings _____ .

24. One's parents _____ .

25. I get tired _____ .

26. I am dependent upon _____ .

27. If things go wrong I _____ .

28. When I was a child _____ .

29. I want my children to _____ .

30. I get a lift from _____ .

REGISTRATION FORM

Name: _____ Spouse's name: _____

Address: _____ Phone: _____

Occupation: _____ Spouse's Occupation: _____

Name and Ages of Children   School

_____   _____

_____   _____

_____   _____

_____   _____

_____   _____

Intended goal you wish to attain through this program:

Some topics I would like to discuss in the group are:

Evaluation to be Completed at End of Program

1. What did you like best about the program?

2. What did you dislike?

3. Do you feel you accomplished your goal?

4. Did your goal change during the program?

5. Do you feel that additional meetings would be helpful?

6. Other suggestions or comments:

ATTENDANCE SHEET

Parent Group _____

Meeting Date _____

Meeting No. _____

Name & Address	Phone	1	2	3	4	5	6	7	8	9	10	11	12	13	14	15

SAMPLE LETTER OF INVITATION FOR PARENTS

Date

Dear Parent:

We are very pleased to invite your participation in a parent discussion group that will focus on "Helping Parents to Help Their Children." The sessions will deal with the basic developmental tasks faced by all children and problems related to their achievement. (*Optional sentence:* However, special attention will be given to issues concerning children with learning disabilities.)

We hope you will plan to attend the first meeting, to be held on *date* at *time* in *room* at *place*. Our psychologist will lead these meetings, and will be glad to address your concerns and any questions you may have. The meetings will continue over fifteen sessions, and only twelve to sixteen parents can be accepted for this group. However, a new group plans to meet in the spring. Please indicate your interest by completing the bottom of this page and returning it to us by *date*. For best results we strongly recommend that both husband and wife attend the sessions together. We look forward to meeting you.

Sincerely,

_____

Parent Response

Please check appropriate category:

_____ Yes, we will attend the group meetings.

_____ Yes, I will attend the group meetings.

_____ Yes, I am/we are interested, but can only attend days or nights (*circle one*). Please provide other group meeting times.

_____ Yes, I am interested in attending the spring group.

_____ I am not interested in attending any group.

Name: _____ Phone: _____

Address: _____

Comments/Questions: _____

Human Relations Training: Identification of Feelings

Focus on Listening for the Feeling

1. List as many "good feeling" words as you can think of in one minute.
2. List as many "bad feeling" words as you can think of in one minute.

Identify the Feeling in The Following Statements

1. I can't tie my shoe.
2. I wish there was no school today, Mommy.
3. I hate to practice.
4. Oh, do I have to come in right now?
5. Mommy, will you come up to bed with me?
6. I don't want to clean up my plate.
7. I can't find my sweater.
8. Someone ripped my jacket.
9. I hate the police lady . . . she's always yelling and saying "hurry up!"
10. Do you have to go out tonight?
11. Why do I have to shut off the TV?
12. Daddy is mean . . . I don't care if he doesn't take me with him.
13. John is always hitting me.
14. This is too hard . . . I can't finish it.
15. I won't wear my rubbers. I just won't.
16. Why do I have to go to sleep so early?
17. What will you do to me if I break it?
18. Why can't Daddy live at home?
19. Teachers are always yelling, "Finish your work!"

20. How come we don't have a boat . . . Johnnie's father has one.
21. I know you are listening but you're not hearing me!

Exercise in Distinguishing Content from Feelings

The leader presents the following statements and asks the parents which word best describes the content and which describes the feelings.

It's not the endless housework that gets to me, it's just that no one seems to notice whether it's done or not.

- disappointment
- unloved
- unimportant

That kid's crying really gets to me. Even when I know she has a reason, I just can't stand her crying!

- frustration
- despair

My stomach caved in when I heard that scream. All I could think of was, "What's happened now?"

- fear
- helplessness
- anger

We just couldn't believe our eyes! Joey, our Joey, petting that puppy! I guess that behavior modification treatment really works. Why just a few weeks ago he'd be running and screaming at the sight of any dog.

- surprise
- relief
- pleasure
- delight
- satisfaction

We found just the right house. I can't believe we're finally going to have enough room to spread out.

- happiness
- relief
- delight

Dinner is pandemonium. Everyone buzzes around, picking at this and that, screaming, yelling, teasing, asking, "When will it be ready?" I hardly know what I'm doing, and I almost want to chuck the whole thing and leave.

- exhaustion
- anger
- frustration
- overwhelming confusion

I had shopped, oh, for hours to find just the right jacket that the kid wanted. Then when I bought it and brought it home he just would not wear it! Never even could tell me why he wouldn't wear it. Wouldn't even try it on!

- disappointment
- frustration
- anger

If only they'd just pick up their own clothes. I just wouldn't mind doing the regular housework—washing, cleaning, shopping—if only they would show just a little consideration for me.

- hopelessness
- disappointment
- unloved

You should hear my neighbor. Her kids can do no wrong. It's really a pain to hear her brag when you know they're real hellions at other people's houses. I feel like telling her to buzz off.

- envy
- annoyance
- anger

The baby was crying, the phone was ringing, the other kid came in with a bleeding knee, and I just felt paralyzed. It was awful—what to attend to first?

- overwhelmed
- helplessness
- fear

Gee, how does she do it? Seven kids and a big house and she can talk about getting a day off every week to spend on herself.

- admiration
- envy
- apprehension

That kid wouldn't pick up a book if you paid him. He'll listen to me read—he'll even ask me to read—but he doesn't even try!

- frustration
- confusion
- helplessness

I could see he was close to tears, but I just had to make him understand he can't get away with taking things that don't belong to him.

- sympathy
- bafflement
- concern

I tried to comfort her, but she cried inconsolably, and I just stood there. She wouldn't even let me put my arm around her.

- helplessness
- sympathy
- bafflement

Oh, I just dread meal time. No matter what I serve, that kid will pick and whine, and leave most of it. As bad as that is, then I have the problem of stopping her from snacking.

- anger
- helplessness
- anxiety

For no reason at all, I found myself screaming at that kid. He was playing with his little cars—not really making any unusual noise, but after the day I'd had and all the pounding in my head, I couldn't help it. But I just can't forget how the poor kid looked at me. I was unfair to him.

- guilt
- regret
- sadness

Identifying Statements in Terms of Additive, Subtractive,
or Interchangeable Qualities

Each of these statements has two to three responses. Please identify the feeling expressed in the statement. Then indicate whether the responses are *additive, subtractive, interchangeable.* The samples are based on *Human Relations Training: A Manual for Trainers* by Sydnor, Akridge, and Parkhill (1972).

1. I can't believe he doesn't understand how hard I've tried to make our marriage work. I really feel sick that he can't see all that I've done.

    a. You should have tried harder. Now you'll just have to face the consequences. (−)

    b. You're really feeling disappointed—it's really terrible that he doesn't recognize your efforts!   (=)

2. She said, "You're huge you know. You're just too fat." I stood there dismayed. I couldn't believe my own mother would say something like that, I just didn't know what to say!

a. You really feel hurt because your mother was so blunt, and because she called you huge. (=)

b. Well, you really are fat you know! (−)

3. I went up to talk to my son's teacher, and the right words just wouldn't come. I felt, well, I just couldn't say anything. She was so cold and so forbidding, I didn't know what to do. I knew what I wanted to say, but I couldn't.

a. You were confused. (−)

b. You must have felt intimidated because she seemed impossible to reach . . . like you were talking to a wall. (+)

4. I guess it would be better to just let him fall flat on his face, but he's the only kid I have!

a. You feel bad to see him getting hurt, and you feel like you want to protect him even though you know that will not really help him because in the end he has to do things for himself. (+)

b. Do you feel the need to protect and shield him even though you know it's wrong? (=)

c. I guess you are just going to have to learn that you can't live his life for him. (−)

5. Meeting people is really hard for me. I just don't know what to say. I just seem to stand there like a lump—and I really wish I could be friendly.

a. When you meet people you really feel stupid and awkward. (=)

b. Meeting people makes you feel self-conscious and tongue-tied even though you'd really want to be liked by them. (+)

c. You're really not very good with people, are you? (−)

Based on Human Relations Training; A Programmed Manual, *by Sydnor, Akridge, and Parkhill. Minde, La.*

SAMPLE ROLE-PLAYING SITUATIONS

1. Mary is getting dressed and discovers a rip in her favorite jeans. There is no time to mend them and she declares she won't go to school until you fix them for her.

2. You have helped Susie to get ready for her friend's birthday party but she has been dawdling and when she is finally ready, she decides she can't go because it's too late.

3. You have spent the whole afternoon helping your child select a suitable jacket. Finally, it looks as if he found one that fits him, and that he likes. When you get it home, he won't wear it because he says his old one is more comfortable.

4. Karen's progress report from her teacher reveals that the reason for poor grades is her lack of attention in class. You would like to get Karen's viewpoint on this. When you ask her about it she says she hates school and starts to cry.

5. You find that your little girl is generally excluded by her friends in school. You feel bad about it and try to discuss it with her. She tells you she doesn't like her school friends because they are mean.

6. Your husband has instructed eight-year-old Jerry to remain in his room for an hour because of a minor problem. Your six-year-old comes to you and reports that Jerry is not in his room, but is working on a model in the basement.

7. Your husband announces he has two tickets to the hockey game. He decides to take the oldest child first because she is interested in hockey. Your second oldest, who has started to play hockey, is crushed and protests vigorously, saying that she is "just a girl" and that he should be the one to go. He cries and cries piteously.

8. Your little girl has been watching the muscular dystrophy program on TV, in which one of the children has passed on. She turns to you and asks, "What's it like to die? Does everyone go to heaven?" (A child in your family died the previous year, leaving her the youngest.)

9. You have promised to take Richard to Toyland upon completing your morning's chores. Your best friend arrives with her two children, whom Richard normally likes. Suddenly Richard is very hostile and uncooperative. When she leaves, he refuses to go with you.

10. Carol promised John her package of M&Ms if he would help her wipe the dishes. John finished wiping the dishes and found that she had eaten half the package. John is angry and crying and starts to strike her.

11. You are helping your little girl to dry her hair in front of the mirror. Suddenly she blurts out, "I wish I was pretty."

12. Your boy comes home very despondent and seemingly discouraged. When you ask him what the matter is he responds in a loud and angry voice, "*Nothing*!!"

WHAT'S A PARENT TO DO?

When a child seems to be causing more than her share of trouble, do you

- consider why she's trying to get your undivided attention?
- try to discover the reason behind the noise?
- avoid comparing her to anyone else—except herself in better behaved days?
- count to ten before punishing—and correct her in a quiet voice?

When a child makes a mistake, do you

- avoid treating her carelessness as an intentional misdeed?
- let her know that "everyone makes mistakes," and that she can profit from them?

When a child balks at doing household chores, do you

- make sure she understands what's expected of her?
- assure her that she's needed as a family member?
- insist quietly and pleasantly that she finish her chores right away, before playing?

When a child gets rough, and frequently fights with other children, especially her siblings, do you

- make a firm and definite statement of disapproval?
- quickly give them another outlet for their energies (helping you, checking the flower garden, getting the mail)?

When a child seems burdened by too many rules, do you

- explain that you make rules because you love her?
- try to minimize the number of rules, but enforce the rules you make?
- make sure you have a good reason for each rule?

Parent-Child Interaction

A Family at Dinner

Mother to Father	How was your day?
Father	Oh . . . we . . . uh . . . look at that kid . . . picking up the meat with his hands!
Mother	When will you learn to use the manners we've taught you?
Child	Why? What's wrong? I didn't do nothing.
Father	Gosh, he can't even speak English. Why is he going to school?
Mother	Oh, he can. He's just got to be like all the rest—teenage horrors!
Child	See! I can't do anything right! You're always criticizing me, picking my friends apart. That's why I hate to eat with you.
Mother	Would I be criticizing you if you were doing the right thing? Why do you have to make every meal a horror show? Your father is tired when he comes home. Don't you ever think about anyone else except yourself?
Father	Oh, let's not blow everything up into a big lecture. I'd like to have one peaceful meal!
Mother	Who's blowing what up? You're the one who started everything. I was only trying to back you up, and here you are criticizing me! What's with you?
Child	Yeah, Ma, you're always on my back. Even Dad can see that!
Father	I only spoke to him because I know you hate his manners. I was trying to back you up. *To the child:* Now you stop harassing your mother.
Mother	Oh, I give up. Let's just forget the whole thing.

What happened? How was the father feeling? the mother? the child? Identify the family alignments. Who is being scapegoated?

PROBLEM-SOLVING TECHNIQUES

1. Listen attentively to the feelings behind the words.

2. Indicate your concern and respond to the feelings without criticizing or shaming the child.

3. Invite child's participation into exploring possible options available to him for solving his problem.

4. Share your ideas, but do not limit his exploration.

5. If child's solution is obviously destructive to himself or to others, reflect your concern and indicate that you cannot permit or give your permission to that particular action, but that you will continue to help him find another solution.

Teaching Behaviors

1. Do you understand your child—know her cues. Know what is age-appropriate so you will not get anxious and put things out of perspective.

2. Have faith in her ability to grow and understand so you will not worry that she is not like every other kid.

3. Listen to what she says and does.

4. Understand and respond to the feelings expressed or implied.

5. Help her to search for solutions to her difficulties, first by helping her to think things through and then by sharing ideas. Do not present her with ready solutions.

6. Encourage and develop her self-confidence and self-esteem by praise and acceptance, and show real pleasure in her being.

7. Never make her ashamed of her feelings, but help her to understand and sort them out so she can be in control of them.

8. Encourage independence so that she can develop a sense of competence.

9. Be understanding of her fears (even when they seem unreasonable) so that she can learn to deal with them.

10. Encourage peer interaction so that she can learn to relate to others and to give and take.

11. Encourage respect for authority by being approachable and willing to consider her point of view.

Appendix B
Materials and Handouts Related
to Learning Disabilities
and Speech Problems

CHAPTER 766
MY RIGHTS AND RESPONSIBILITIES AS A PARENT

Within the regulations of Chapter 766 (Massachusetts State Law), I have the following rights and responsibilities as a parent:

1. to be informed in writing that a referral has been made
2. to know who made the referral
3. to be informed of the nature of the evaluation process and the types of assessments indicated for my child
4. to request a "full" evaluation of my child, if needed (this consists of five or more assessments)
5. my permission must be obtained in writing before any evaluation or placement can take place; and I have the right to change my mind
6. to know the date(s) of the evlauation(s)
7. to meet with the chairperson of the TEAM prior to the evaluation
8. my child has the right to meet and to participate if he/she is at least fourteen years of age
9. a home visit, if necessary, will be made with my permission
10. to be present at all meetings
11. to participate in all meetings where my child's program is being discussed, developed and written
12. to be accompanied and represented by an individual of my choice (i.e., lawyer, child advocate, etc.)
13. meetings will be held at mutually convenient times and places
14. IEP or recommendation of "no special education" shall be completed within 30 school days after the date of consent
15. to obtain an independent evaluation at the school's expense (if obtained from an "approved facility"). This independent evaluation may consist of the same or less than all of the assessments done in the original evaluation.

This form is used by the Medford, Massachusetts, Public Schools to inform parents of their rights under Massachusetts Chapter 766, Public Law 94-142.

LEARNING DISABILITY TERMS

Note: These are capsule identifications and should not be considered full descriptions of any learning disability. Be sure that any terms used in the diagnosis of your child are fully explained by your doctor or specialist.

ataxia Abnormal (meaning below average) muscular control.

dyscalculia The inability to grasp mathematical concepts with normal teaching.

dysgraphia Difficulty with writing.

dyslexia The inability to read with understanding.

hyperactivity (or **hyperkinesis**) Abnormally increased motor activity; constant movement without apparent purpose. Can also refer to excessive verbal responses.

hypoactivity (or **hypokinesis**) An abnormally quiescent state; unresponsiveness; tendency to withdraw; inattention to stimuli.

maturational lag Lack or slowness of a child's neurological development.

minimal brain dysfunction (**MBD**) A minor neurological malfunction that prevents sensory stimuli from being properly processed by the brain. Some experts find the term out of date, or contend that it is used too generally in order to avoid identifying more specific learning disorders.

perceptually handicapped Being unable to recognize or to become aware of certain words, objects, and other data through the senses (sight, hearing, touch, taste, and smell).

strephosymbolia The reversal of symbols as they are found in reading and writing ("was" for "saw," for example).

Children with Learning Disabilities

Who Is This Child?

Usually . . .

- This is an intelligent child who fails at school.

- This is the child who at school age reads *on* for *no,* writes *41* for *14,* *p* for *d* or *q* for *b,* and can't remember the sequence of letters that make up a word.

- This is the child who loses her homework, misplaces her book, does not know what day it is, or what year, or what season.

- This is the child who calls breakfast *lunch;* who is confused by *yesterday, today,* and *tomorrow;* the child whose timing is always off.

Frequently . . .

- This is the child who can't picture things in his mind, who can't visualize or remember what he sees.

- This is the quiet child who bothers nobody in the classroom but does not learn.

- This is the older child whose language comes out jumbled; who stops and starts in the middle of a sentence or an idea; . . . who talks about hospitals, animals, and enemies.

Sometimes . . .

- This is the child who can add and multiply but not subtract or divide . . . who can do math in his head but can't write it down.

- This is the child who skips words, omits them, or adds them when he is reading aloud.

From No Easy Answers: The Learning Disabled Child at Home and at School, *Sally L. Smith, Author, Bantam paperback, 1981. Reprinted with permission.*

No Easy Answers

The Learning Disabled Child
Is a Child with Disorder

Usually, the child with an intact nervous system is a well-organized little human being by school age. He has sorted, classified, categorized information into the proper mail boxes in his mind. He has achieved the maturation necessary to learn efficiently. By age six, most youngsters are ready for formal education. The child is ready for teaching. His equipment can handle it; he has the tools to do the job.

The learning disabled youngster is not ready on time. He is disorganized. He is consumed by *disorder*. He is immature rather than abnormal. A doctor would say that he suffers from neurological immaturity or minimal brain dysfunction. An educator would say that he has a learning disability. A parent would say: "Something is wrong."

The learning disabled child can't make sense of what he receives through his senses, even though his sight, hearing, and other sense organs are all intact. The messages he receives are jumbled—scattered all over the place. He is distractable, which most people think is not paying attention. But, in fact, he is paying too much attention to too many things. At age seven or eight he is frequently very similar in his social behavior to the two- and three-year-old. He craves center stage—not out of any base ambitions but because of immaturity. He seems to need constant recognition of his existence long after the preschool years are over. Because of his many difficulties (with tying shoe laces, organization of speech, reading), he is dependent longer on the adults around him and must call for help over a longer period of time. The need for attention may equal the need for help, and many a learning disabled youngster has cleverly discovered that helplessness brings swift attention. Also, there are many children who would so much rather receive negative attention than no attention that they will purposely get in trouble or "act out" to evoke an adult response. Often they would rather be thought of as "bad" than "dumb." Some youngsters will provoke trouble with other children to make sure they are not ignored; they can then complain about being teased or picked on, but they have been the center of everyone's attention. This happens frequently with learning disabled youngsters.

From No Easy Answers: The Learning Disabled Child at Home and at School, *Sally L. Smith, Author, Bantam paperback, 1981. Reprinted with permission.*

The Learning Disabled Youngster Tends to Become Rigid and Inflexible

He is reminiscent of a very young child who cannot deal with alternatives at the immature level of his age. He becomes anxious when he is taken to the park by a new, unfamiliar route. He is upset on a Sunday morning when his parents have breakfast in their pajamas—breaking the known routine of dress first, breakfast afterward. He won't accept a broken cookie, because a cookie is round; if the broken piece is jagged, it can't be a cookie. He does not recognize a teacher outside of school. He may appear paralyzed when faced with two equal choices, unable to select either one.

The inflexible child who wants what he wants when he wants it, no matter what is going on around him—a storm, a riot, an accident, a crisis—he is the same child who doesn't see the wholeness of things. He gets caught up in the details and misses the big picture.

Lost in Time and Space

The learning disabled child is most often lost in space—lost in up–down, left–right, above–below, top–bottom, in–out, into–out of, under–over, apart–together. He does not automatically know how to operate in space; he cannot visualize spaces. How can he know where the top shelf is if he is not sure that his feet are below his head?

He can't remember where to go, frequently gets lost, loses not only himself but his possessions, and does not see things that are right in front of his nose. Often when he is asked to stand in front of his desk, he stands behind it. Frequently he is asked to put the paper into the box, he puts it under the box.

This is why clearly defined spaces, or small spaces, spell safety to the learning disabled child. This is why security depends on the same seat at the dining-room table, the same place in the car, the same chair at school. A learning disabled child usually has a poor image of his own body. He does not connect the parts to the whole body. He does not know how far it extends or how much space it takes up. His development in this respect lags way behind what is usual for his chronological age. Frequently the learning disabled child is awkward and clumsy.

Clumsiness is

- misjudging—overdoing; underdoing; off balance
- poor timing—too fast, too slow
- not looking
- not listening
- not being able to coordinate several things at once

Free Spirit

There is a sheer job—temporary though it may be—that many a learning disabled child brings to life. He seems to embrace life with an enthusiasm and jauntiness that most of us

From No Easy Answers: The Learning Disabled Child at Home and at School, *Sally L. Smith, Author, Bantam paperback, 1981. Reprinted with permission.*

lose with maturity. The spontaneous expression of feeling, the unedited comment, and the untrampled-upon gesture are all trademarks of the impulsive child. There is a freshness which he conveys, perhaps because he does not see the whole picture, that turns our attention to experiences we have come to take for granted. In the midst of checking the route map, watching the road signs, estimating when the next gas stop must be made, our attention is suddenly diverted to an unexpected delight when the learning disabled child remarks: "How fresh and good the grass smells!" With all the heartache he feels and brings into his home, he often touches the family with a freshness, a pure, natural quality.

Their School Problems

Learning disabled children need to be taught how to learn. Their reading, spelling, and arithmetic skills often range from considerably below to far below the norm. Frequently their spoken language, thinking, and behavior are also extremely delayed.

Teddy lost everything. He lost his pencil. He lost his homework. He lost himself going from one classroom to another. He lost interest in the middle of a project. And he lost his memory for the words that he could read perfectly well yesterday.

Katie said: "I don't want to read. You can't make me!"

Andy was a good boy. He was quiet and well-mannered in class. He was a whiz at sports. But he could not speak well. It was so embarrassing for him to talk that his teacher let him read silently, rather than aloud in front of the class, and missed the fact that he could not read at all.

"How's school?" is the question all grownups ask. That's where the child is expected to "deliver the goods" in a productive society.

No matter how much they love him, parents take the child's failure as their own. So they try by every means possible to make him do better. They tell him, as his teacher has told him before, that he is not trying . . . , that he is not trying enough, that he's too used to getting his own way, that it's time for him to stop being a baby and grow up and to take responsibility by *learning to read*. They talk to him at length. They bribe and punish, spend hours going over his schoolwork with him. And they can't understand why all that extra effort doesn't bring him more success with the written word.

From No Easy Answers: The Learning Disabled Child at Home and at School, *Sally L. Smith, Author, Bantam paperback, 1981. Reprinted with permission.*

TO READ...A CHILD NEEDS:

SYMBOLISM-VERBAL SKILLS
- vocabulary
- comprehension-understanding of concepts expressed in words
- verbal reasoning
- recognizing the oneness of objects, symbols, words-separate identities
- understanding that a mark, a sound, a pattern, represent an object or idea

RHYTHM
TIMING
SENSE OF TIME

• ORGANIZATION of THOUGHT • ORDER •
- ability to sort information classify, categorize, label.
- appropriateness (what belongs, what's missing)
- ability to recognize parts that make up a whole
- ability to break down the whole into parts
- recognize sequences •

first
next
last

beginning
middle
end

small
big
bigger

AUDITORY PERCEPTION
- listening skills
- discrimination
- memory
- sequential memory
- understanding

TACTILE PERCEPTION
- discrimination
- memory
- understanding

SELF CONTROL TO SUSTAIN ATTENTION

SPACIAL RELATIONSHIPS AND SPACING
- left to right progression from right
- knowing left from right
- eye-hand-foot coordination in space
- directionality
- directions in space
- judgment planning— (motor planning) sequencing

EYE TRACKING

EYE, HAND, AND FOOT COORDINATION

VISUAL PERCEPTION
- observation skills
- discrimination
- memory memory
- sequential memory
- understanding to give meaning

form constancy
figure ground
size
shape
color

INTEGRATING SEVERAL PROCESSES AT ONCE

INTEGRATING SOUND & SIGHT TO HAVE MEANING

Figure B-1. *What a Child Needs to Read*

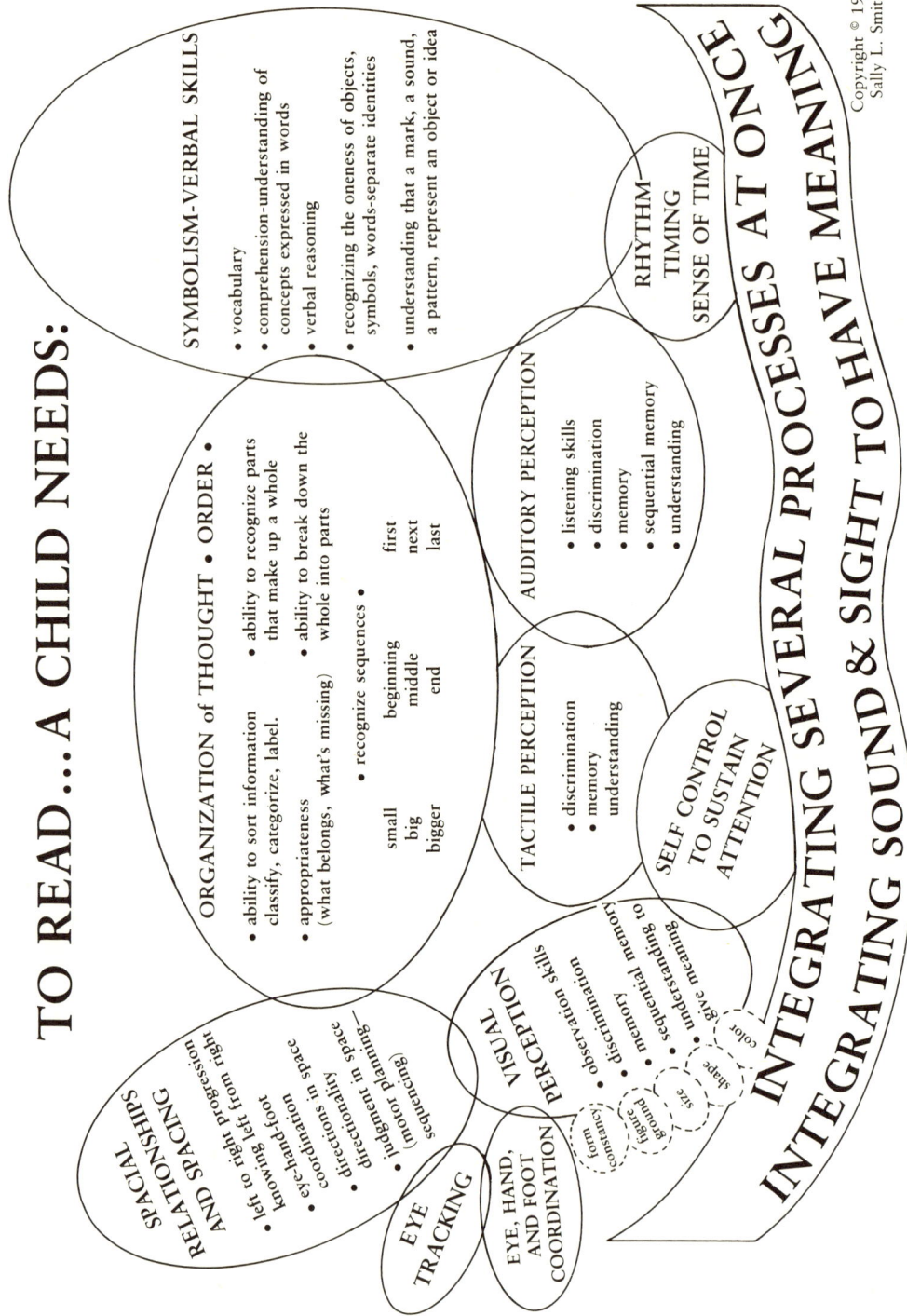

Source: *No Easy Answers: The Learning Disabled Child at Home and at School*, Sally L. Smith, author, Bantam Paperback, 1981. Reprinted with permission.

DIVIDE   MULTIPLY
IN | GROUPS   IN | GROUPS
SUBTRACT   ADD
BACKWARD   FORWARD
LESS   COUNTING   MORE

TO DO ARITHMETIC

SORTING ··· DIFFERENTIATING ··· INTEGRATING
INTEGRATING ··· DIFFERENTIATING ··· SORTING ··· SEQUENCING

A CHILD NEEDS:

MEMORY
• To hold several things at once in the mind

REASON   SYMBOLISM
Induce   • Simple association
Deduca   • Concept of oneness
           (1 – 1 correspondence)
           • A numeral = a quantity
           • The role of zero

PART-WHOLE RELATIONSHIPS

GROUPING & REGROUPING
(Comparisons)

SWITCHING
From one process to another,
One combination to another

Understanding
EQUALS & EQUIVALENTS
Form—Constancy—Conservation

MORE THAN/LESS THAN

• EYE TRACKING
• EYE-HAND COORDINATION
• VISUALIZING THE PROCESS

VISUAL-SPACIAL PERCEPTION

DIRECTIONALISM

Left Vertical Top	Right Horizontal Bottom
Position in Space	Place Value
+ ×	1,2,3; 123
13 31	$150; $1.50

AUDITORY PERCEPTION
Following Directions
Sequential Memory
TIMING
1st, Next, Last

SELF-CONTROL

TO SUSTAIN ATTENTION

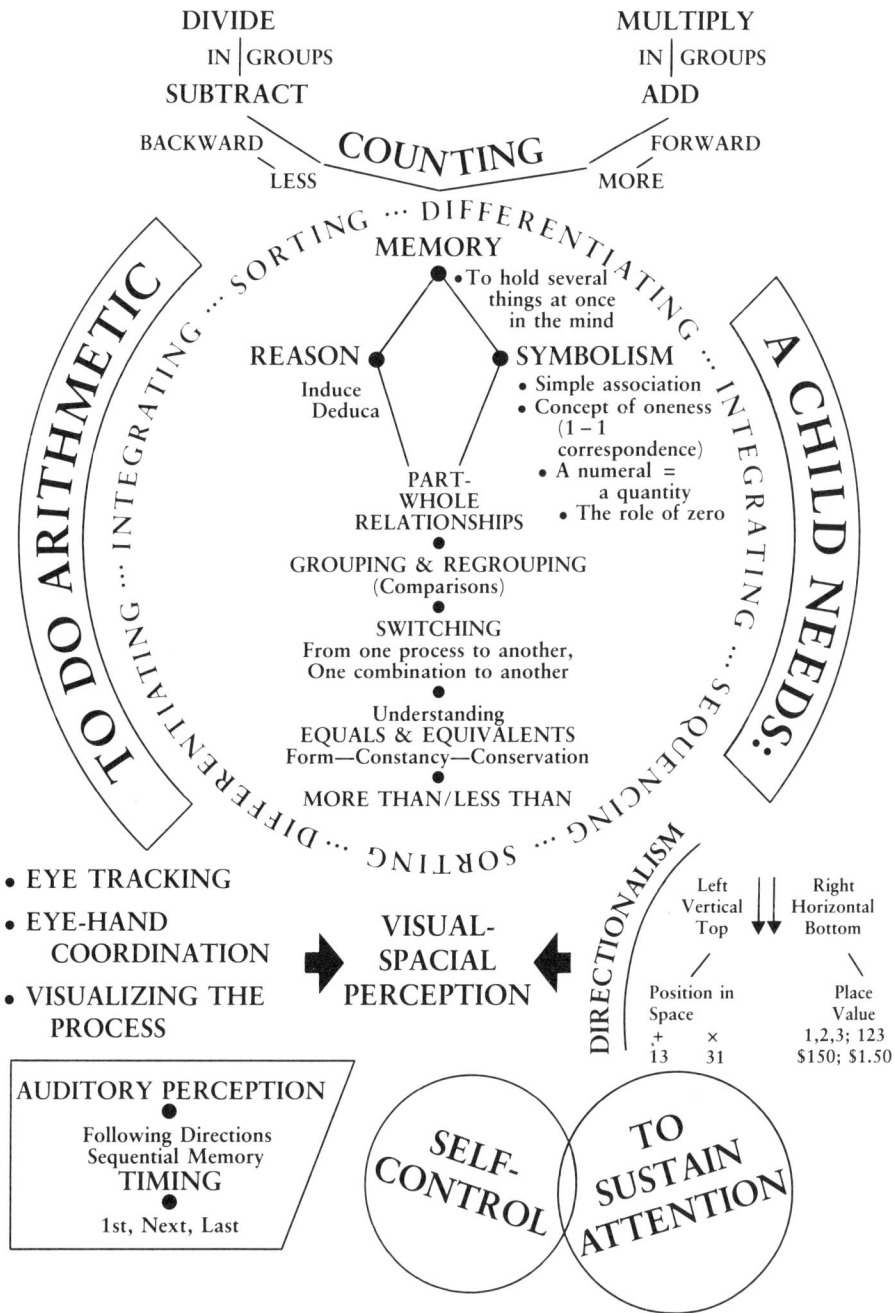

Source: *No Easy Answers: The Learning Disabled Child at Home and at School,* Sally L. Smith, author, Bantam Paperback, 1981. Reprinted with permission.

Figure B–2. *What a Child Needs to Do Arithmetic*

Why Is a Child Learning Disabled?

It is not because the parents have not tried. It is not because the parents do not care. It is not because the child is stubborn. It is not because the child is dull. It is not because the child is lazy. It is not because the child is spoiled.

There is no known simple explanation why a child has learning disabilities—there is no one cause. There seem to be many causes that are responsible for learning disabilities.

Before birth

- maternal malnutrition
- bleeding in pregnancy
- poor placental attachment to the uterus
- toxemia in pregnancy
- infectious disease of pregnant mother (German measles, a viral disease, influenza, or a chronic disease)
- alcoholism during pregnancy
- the taking of certain drugs during pregnancy
- Rh incompatibility.

During birth

- long or difficult delivery producing anoxia (not enough oxygen in the brain)
- prematurity
- cord around neck or breech delivery
- poor position in the uterus
- dry birth where the water broke prematurely
- intracranial pressure at the time of birth due to forceps delivery or a narrow pelvic arch in the mother
- rapid delivery exposing the infant too quickly to a new air pressure.

From No Easy Answers: The Learning Disabled Child at Home and at School, *Sally L. Smith. Author, Bantam paperback, 1981. Reprinted with permission.*

After birth

- length of time to produce breathing after birth (often occurs with prematurity, difficult delivery, or twins)
- high fever at any early age
- sharp blow to head from fall or accident
- meningitis or encephalitis
- lead poisoning
- drug intoxication
- oxygen deprivation due to suffocation, respiratory distress, breath holding, or severe nutritional deficiences.

Heredity

- there are many families in which reading disabilities can be traced through several generations. Usually the father, an uncle, or other relatives had the problem.

It is not worth agonizing over which of these factors produced the problems of a particular child. It might be something not even mentioned here, as yet unknown! Placing blame, pointing an accusing finger, feeling overwhelmed with guilt, giving way to fear that some thoughtless action produced a child's learning problems have all never been found to help parents help children with the problem. Sometimes it temporarily helps teachers (who feel totally frustrated by the learning disabled child) to blame parents, but that does not help the children either. Teachers, like parents, usually wish to do the best they can for each child and often seek an easy, quick remedy. The causes of learning disability are beyond teacher control as they are beyond parental control.

From No Easy Answers: The Learning Disabled Child at Home and at School, *Sally L. Smith, Author, Bantam paperback, 1981. Reprinted with permission.*

Parents' Feelings

Exasperated . . . puzzled . . . uncertain . . . frantic . . . exhausted . . . helpless . . . hopeful. These are the feelings of the parents of a learning disabled child. She is bewildering. She drains parents and teachers. When they are with such a child, adults who are otherwise competent feel helpless and inadequate.

It is hard for any parents to accept the fact that they have a learning disabled child; for some it becomes an almost overwhelming tragedy.

There are stages that parents go through with their perfectly normal looking, intelligent child, who does not learn or behave as other children her age do. A whole gamut of emotions must be faced before parents can grapple effectively with the stark truth of a child having learning disabilities. There is no set order to these feelings. Usually they start with denial and, most often, end with acceptance and hope.

Denial. "My child doesn't really have anything wrong with her. She only needs more time, more understanding neighbors, a better teacher, or a better school. These people don't understand her. She's just the way I was. There's nothing basically wrong."

Flight. "These doctors jump to conclusions. We're going to see another specialist. They're only out to make money with more tests and more examinations. We have to fly to the east (or the west). There's a new specialist with a good reputation."

Isolation. "Why doesn't anyone care? Nobody seems to understand. Why can't they make allowances? She's much more interesting and unique than most children."

Guilt. "What did I do to her? Why is God punishing me? How could I have made life better for her? If only I hadn't let her bump her head—if only I had kept her from catching measles—if only I had been more strict."

Anger. "Doctors don't know anything! They should have caught it earlier! That teacher is out of her mind! These psychologists are for the birds! I hate this neighborhood. That child makes a monkey out of me!"

Blame. "You baby her. You're the one who spoils her. You don't make her take responsibility. We never had anything like this on my side of the family."

Fear. "Maybe it's worse than they say. Is she retarded and they won't tell me? Is it a progressive disease? Will she ever be able to marry, have children, or hold a job?"

From No Easy Answers: The Learning Disabled Child at Home and at School, *Sally L. Smith, Author, Bantam paperback, 1981. Reprinted with permission.*

Envy. "Look at those other kids. They don't know how lucky they are. Everything comes easily to them. How did they become so popular? We're better parents. It's not fair!"

Bargaining. Maybe she'll be OK if we move. Maybe she'll do fine in third grade. Maybe if we send her to camp she'll shape up. Maybe if I work with her every night she'll be OK. Maybe if she goes to visit her grandparents she'll pick up. Maybe if . . ."

Depression. "I've failed her. I'm no good. No wonder she can't make it. I can't either. The world's no good. I'm no good. There's no hope."

Mourning. "Think what could have been. She might have . . ."

Acceptance and hope. "OK So she's got learning disabilities. What can I do to help? How can I make her feel better about herself? What are her strengths? What are her interests? We'll make it! It will just take time and some cooperative efforts.

OK So your child has learning disabilities! As a parent you have the same choices your child has—to pity yourself or to do the best with what you have and work hard at it.

Can a learning disabled youngster make it in the adult world? Most of them grow up to be achievers. Many youngsters never excel in reading, and a huge number are poor spellers, but they still become successful in business, mechanical fields, architecture, the arts, and many other occupations. Some become exceptionally creative, imaginative problem solvers (while others, of course, do not). Some have become doctors, scientists, inventors, politicians, and generals.

Today, more than ever before, there is great hope that a learning disabled child will be able to function effectively in our society. We know so much more than we did previously. More professionals, as well as parents, are becoming alert to the problem of the learning disabled child earlier in her life. Some years ago a youngster's problems would not be recognized until the sixth grade, unless they were very severe or combined with disruptive behavior. Now they are likely to draw attention in the second or third grade, and it certainly should be no later. Most services are becoming available to both the children and their families.

If, by the second grade, a child is really not doing well, and if a good deal of what has been described earlier can be recognized, it may be worthwhile at this point for her parents to seek competent professional help. They should find the diagnostic center near them that knows the most about learning disabilities and have the child tested.

If there is no diagnostic center close enough, they should try to find a psychologist whose speciality is testing and who knows the evidence of learning disabilities. It is important that the results be interpreted to the parents in detail. Here are some of the questions they might want to ask: What are my child's strengths? What are my child's weaknesses? Is a neurological examination advised? Will educational treatment alone be enough? Does my child need a tutor? Does she need a speech therapist? Does she, or do we as a total family, need psychological counseling? Is any further testing by medical specialists needed? Does she need medication? Which has top priority? And why? What can the school do? And how can we tell them what to do? What can we as parents do?

The most important thing a parent can do is provide structure in the child's life— order in her space and sequencing in her time. There needs to be a place for everything

From No Easy Answers: The Learning Disabled Child at Home and at School, *Sally L. Smith, Author, Bantam paperback, 1981. Reprinted with permission.*

in her room. If there are not too many things, it is easier to have a cleared place where each thing can be put away. Shelves are often preferable to drawers because she can see her things in their proper place, rather than having to visualize what is in a drawer. Structure can be introduced into her time by making her fully familiar with the parts of each of her usual routines—what comes first, next, and last.

It is obvious that all children need as much positive reinforcement for their good efforts as they can get. The need to be rewarded whenever they succeed with praise, a gesture, or some form of approval. But even the best of parents cannot salvage the ego of the child who has failed and failed again in school, in the neighborhood, and on the athletic field. Often a tutor, a special class, or a special school are necessary to provide the therapy needed to make this child feel competent, to show her that she is capable of doing something about herself, that she is the master of her own destiny.

The defeat that is so often met by a learning disabled child can make it hard for her to develop a strong sense of self, and there are times when it is necessary for parents to consult a psychologist or psychiatrist. It is the job of these professionals to help build the ego strength so vitally needed for every child's development. Sometimes play therapy; sometimes an individual therapist who talks with the child; sometimes group therapy can help a child. These methods can help her parents, too, to cope with the reality of living with learning disabilities. The fears, the anger, the guilt, the anxiety that are suffered by both the child and her parents can become better understood and thereby eased. If a child feels victimized by her learning disabilities, or seems totally unmanageable or very depressed, these are the times when it is frequently necessary to consult a professional counselor. To locate a counselor, one might begin by checking with the local Association for Children with Learning Disabilities (ACLD). See the section "Helpful National Organizations."

There are many psychologists and psychiatrists, even today, who do not know much about learning disabilities. Parents need to be aware of this, because a learning disabled child needs structure in her therapy just as parents need to find out if a therapist understands the unique problems of learning disabled youngsters.

Parents should ask questions such as the following:

- What do you look for to decide whether or not a learning disabled child needs therapy?
- How would you explain the purpose of therapy to a learning disabled child?
- How do you work with the child who has trouble expressing herself in words?
- What can you do with a child who cannot focus her attention?
- Is it effective to work with a child without working with her parents?
- How do you see the relationship of low self-esteem to a child's learning disabilities?
- Under what conditions do you recommend medication?
- Can you explain to me the relationship of learning disabilities to my child's social problems?

It may be that the parents have confidence in the therapist to do an initial evaluation but are not sure that this is a person they trust to work with the child and themselves.

From No Easy Answers: The Learning Disabled Child at Home and at School, *Sally L. Smith, Author, Bantam paperback, 1981. Reprinted with permission.*

An evaluation consists of the therapist meeting with the parents once or twice to take their history and to understand their concerns, having one or two sessions with the child, and then an interpretive session with the parents.

After the diagnostic evaluation, parents have a right to ask the therapist or counselor some questions that will give them an impression of how he or she views their child and to see if the evaluation meshes with their own observations. There should be some new information from the evaluation, but they should also be able to recognize their own child.

A therapist qualified to work with a learning disabled child must be able to answer questions in clear, simple terms because she will be dealing with a child who has difficulty in processing language. If the therapist is vague, obscure, full of technical jargon, is not understanding of or not understandable to the parents, then it is quite likely that she will not be effective with the child either. She also will not be able to give the parents the kind of support they need. If parents do not feel positive toward the therapist, they should set about finding another therapist in whom they can place their confidence. One needs a positive, supportive relationship to proceed with the difficult work ahead. Helping the learning disabled youngster is a joint effort; trust in the therapist is essential to that effort. The therapist who understands learning disabilities can have an enormous impact on the child's behavior at home and at school, and she can have a marked effect on the parents' attitudes and their ability to manage the child. The therapist can affect the comfort and well-being of the whole family.

It is best that parents try not to dwell on the future in their own minds. They can plan realistically for today, tomorrow, next week, even a few months ahead. But it is unrealistic to become preoccupied with the long-range future of a young child. There is not yet enough knowledge; there are too many variables; there are too many unknown factors for this kind of stewing to be in any way useful.

It is vital for them to develop their sense of humor in every way they know how. Laughter helps surmount many a hurdle, and it gives the child a terribly important unspoken message—that life is basically sunny despite all her difficulties. Comical elements can be found in many situations, even though they are sometimes pretty hard to see. When the whole family can see the humor in some of the experiences they go through together, it is really worth it.

From No Easy Answers: The Learning Disabled Child at Home and at School, *Sally L. Smith, Author, Bantam paperback, 1981. Reprinted with permission.*

GROWING UP LEARNING DISABLED

"I can't do anything right. I'm no good. I'm dumb. I'm a retard. Nobody likes me. Everybody's picking on me."

These are some of the feelings that the learning disabled child shoulders as he grows up. He does not understand (or misunderstands) many aspects of his life, and he receives correction or criticism, which he then translates into "everybody's picking on me." It probably reflects his very real view of the situation because he does not interpret the correction or criticism as being helpful. Often, he sees his world as a series of mistakes, one after another, all totaling personal disaster. It is hard to grow up feeling good about himself under these conditions. If he has special skills, a learning disabled child can feel good about his success in sports, his artistic talent, or his popularity with a group. But deep down inside him there is still that gnawing feeling of, "What's really wrong with me?" This is why straight talk is so important. It is vital that the child hear over and over again from different sources that he is intelligent, that he needs more time to learn than others, but that he will make it in the world. He needs as much information about himself as he can handle, and he needs it frequently. He may still feel dumb. But, at least he knows he is not retarded and does not have any progressive brain disease or whatever else he may secretly dread. In many ways, life seems very unfair to him. He perceives the world in the only way he can, and he meets rebuff or ridicule as a result of what he says or does, based on that perception. This youngster is often brought into child guidance clinics because someone thinks he is an angry, willful, unmotivated, or spoiled child who is purposely not performing well at school. This very frightened child cannot, rather than will not, perform well at school.

He is angry at the world's demands on him—demands he cannot meet. He is angry at himself for not being able to do what he wants to do. He is angry at his parents, teachers, brothers, sisters, neighbors, and classmates for seeing him in the act of not being able to achieve. He is angry at God or God's representatives in church or synagogue. He is angry at being what he is.

The delayed maturation keeps this child from acquiring the skills that are needed for independence. He has become a teenager by his number of years; he may have the physical size and pubertal development of a teenager; but his neural development and

From No Easy Answers: The Learning Disabled Child at Home and at School, *Sally L. Smith, Author, Bantam paperback, 1981. Reprinted with permission.*

his behavior are like those of a much younger child. Yet the world expects his behavior to be appropriate for his size.

Independence usually relies on organizational skills. Self-sufficiency means taking responsibility for oneself. In areas where a learning disabled child needs to learn specific everyday skills to enhance his self-reliance, he can be taught to do many of these things, and the feeling of competence he derives from mastery set him up for more accomplishment.

- Use the bus. Learn to go around town; learn the bus insignias, and know their destinations.
- Money. Learn to count change; keep money in a systematic way; make simple accounts.
- Simple cooking. Be able to prepare food; cook eggs and toast; heat soup; make hamburgers, hot dogs, or frozen dinners.
- Time. Learn to read the clock; make approximate schedules; learn the "feel" of intervals of time: How long is 15 minutes? half an hour? two hours?
- Set the table. Lay out correct place settings; clear the table; wash or dry dishes.
- Shopping. Plan purchases; find the right department; make choices.
- Make a bed. Learn the sequence of sheets, blankets, and bed covers; learn tucking-in techniques.
- Newspaper. Know the organization; learn where to find the sports, amusements, want ads, etc.
- Use the telephone. Know how to dial numbers; learn emergency numbers; learn how to ask clear questions; give and receive pertinent information; make an appointment.
- Filling out forms. Learn to fill out a job application, or questionnaires; understand bank forms (use enlarged forms; go slowly, step by step, from very simple—using names only—to more complex).
- Restaurants. Learn how a menu is organized; understand the check; learn to order and to tip.

What Is Really Important?

In the end, what counts are human qualities. A person's sense of himself, his feeling of comfort with himself, and thus his ease with others are what matters. How many adults do you know whose knowledge of spelling or trigonometry makes a difference to you? Does it matter how good your friend's handwriting is or how many historical facts he can recite? Is it important that your friends be athletic and scholarly as well as talented in some artistic field? The chances are that you want to be with a person who is fun and caring. You want a friend who laughs with you, not at you, and who can share your worries as well as your pleasures. You want someone you can count on, whose word is good, who comes through on promises, and who does not keep score on favors given and received. To be a good friend, to be a fine mate, to become a good parent—these are crucial roles in our society and roles that the learning disabled child can fulfill.

From No Easy Answers: The Learning Disabled Child at Home and at School, *Sally L. Smith, Author, Bantam paperback, 1981. Reprinted with permission.*

Helpful National Organizations

All organizations listed here are open to parents, teachers, therapists, and other interested professionals and persons.

Association for Children with Learning Disabilities (ACLD)

Purpose

The ACLD provides information and support, and follows the latest educational and medical research. It also supports legislation for special classes and trained teachers.

Address

To find the organization nearest you, write: ACLD, 5225 Grace Street, Pittsburgh, PA 15236.

Closer Look

Purpose

Closer Look is a national information center operated by the Parents' Campaign for Handicapped Children and Youth. It provides practical advice on how to find educational programs and other kinds of special services.

Address

Closer Look, Box 1492, Washington, DC 20013.

From No Easy Answers: The Learning Disabled Child at Home and at School, *Sally L. Smith, Author, Bantam paperback, 1981. Reprinted with permission.*

National Easter Seal Society

Purpose

The society is a source of information on publications concerning the learning disabled child. It provides clinics, and sponsors research and workshops.

Address

National Easter Seal Society, 2023 West Ogden Avenue, Chicago, IL 60612.

The Council for Exceptional Children (CEC)

Purpose

The council provides an information center for general and specific information on learning disabilities, and publishes useful material.

Address

The Council for Exceptional Children, 1920 Association Drive, Reston, VA 22091.

The Orton Society

Purpose

The society studies preventive measures and treatment for children with specific language disabilities, and sponsors research.

Address

The Orton Society, Inc., 8415 Bellona Lane, Towson, MD 21204.

From No Easy Answers: The Learning Disabled Child at Home and at School, *Sally L. Smith, Author, Bantam paperback, 1981. Reprinted with permission.*

PRACTICAL SUGGESTIONS FOR AT-HOME HELP FOR SPEECH-IMPAIRED CHILDREN

Should I Correct My Child's Speech?

No—not unless your child has established a new sound well enough. When a child begins speech practice at home or in school, she does not know which sound is right or wrong. She can hear, but she does not recognize that her substitutions, omissions, or distortions of sounds are errors. To correct her before she has learned to discriminate which sound should be placed in which word only adds to her frustration.

What Can I Do to Help My Child Learn to Listen and Gain Better Ear Training?

Your own speech patterns should be *slow* and *simple* so that your child has the advantage of hearing the best and clearest speech. When she speaks incorrectly you can repeat the word correctly in the next sentence you say to her. This should be done in an uncritical manner and in the normal course of conversation. Your child might say, "I want *th*ome *th*oup." Your conversation might be, "Yes, we'll get *s*ome *s*oup now. Do you want vegetable *s*oup or chicken *s*oup?" In this way you are bombarding your child's ears with correct speech patterns, without discouragement or making her feel that she has failed.

What Should We Do When We Don't Understand What Our Child Says?

You could act as if you had not heard by simply saying, "I'm sorry, I didn't hear you." This encourages your child to repeat without letting her know that you could not understand her poor speech. Often when a child repeats she attempts to say her words more clearly and this helps her to improve.

Should We Have Home Practice Sessions?

Unguided home practice sessions may do more harm than good. Please *do not* drill with your child unless you have thoroughly discussed your child's problem with a professional.

Please *do not* undertake the task of home sessions unless you have the *time, patience, and understanding* to devote to your child. Remember to consult the speech therapist on whether or not home practice is indicated for your child.

Suggestions For Home Practice Lessons for the Younger Child

1. Set aside a one-minute period for "talking time" three or four times per week. Short lessons conducted at a regular time and place are worth more than an hour inconsistently given. Make a *scrapbook*.

2. Select a time that is likely to be free from interruption. It is helpful if other children can be occupied outdoors, at school, or in another part of the house.

3. Begin with a quick review of the old, familiar, and fun activities. Work for a while in the scrapbook and then carry over the activity without it.

4. Home lessons should be fun—not boring—and try not to *make* your child do something. Your attitude toward practice periods, your individual attention to your child, your curiosity, and observations will help him to want to practice.

5. Be generous with your praise. Encouragement for good performance or even a "good try" is essential for continued interest and learning.

6. Stop the practice session when your child is still interested and getting pleasure from the situations. Do not wait until he is tired.

7. If you are having difficulty do not always assume that your child is being negative. Try to analyze the situation. Why is he reacting this way? Is *your* language level too high? Is the task too difficult? Is your child confused or feeling pressured or meeting failure? Is he ill or fatigued?

8. The purpose and arrangement of the scrapbook are very important for encouraging speech and language development. Children frequently have difficulty organizing their thoughts and recalling appropriate words. Arrange the pages in categories:

- Things I like to eat.
- Things that go.
- Things that make a noise.
- Things to wear.
- Things in the house (by rooms).
- Things that are funny.
- Pets.
- The family.

Questions and Answers

Q. *Why is my child being seen for speech only once a week?*

A. There are at least two reasons. The speech therapist might service between forty and sixty children a week. This overload, as well as the travel time to as many as ten schools, limit the amount of time the children can be seen.

Q. *Why is it that my child has speech for only one-half hour at a time?*

A. A child's attention span for attending to the drills is not more than one-half hour. Also the therapist and the classroom teacher do not want the child to miss more than one-half hour of classwork at one time.

Q. *My child tells me that he played cards in speech today, and last week he played Candyland. What do these games have to do with speech?*

A. In cases where the speech problem is articulation, a child needs an activity that can relax him after extensive drilling. When he plays cards or a game, the rules are changed. Before he can move forward or "go fish" he must attempt to produce his sound correctly. In this way he is motivated to try because the progress of the game depends on it. In areas of language therapy, playing games also serves as motivation.

Puppets are used to increase the amount of speaking that a child does. Matching games are used to teach plurals. Plays are acted out to enable the child to use the language area he finds most difficult.

Q. *How do you teach a child to say a sound correctly?*

A. This is accomplished by following this outline:

Ear training. The child is taught to listen for his special sound, and to tell her when he hears the therapist say it. He is asked to discriminate between the correct and incorrect production of the sound in his own speech and in that of the therapist. The theory behind ear training is that the child cannot produce the sound correctly if he cannot hear the difference between a good and poor sound in others' speech or in his own. Therefore, he cannot correct himself and he continues to produce the incorrect sound.

Production. First a child is taught the correct placement for his tongue, lips, and teeth during the production of the sound. These drills continue throughout therapy; constant reminders for the place of sound production are necessary. A mirror is used to show the child what the correct production looks like, as opposed to how he looks during the incorrect production. The child is taught to produce the sound in isolation at first. Next he learns to say the sound at the beginning of a syllable, then he learns the production at the end of a syllable, and finally in the middle of a syllable. (Middle syllable production is hardest for most children because other sounds precede and follow the target sound.) Word production follows; he is taught to produce a correct sound within a word, and the word is used in a sentence. Finally the child is checked for the amount of carryover of good production into a conversation. Eighty-five percent carryover of correct production is a reasonable goal. At this stage, the child is dismissed from therapy, and rechecked in six months.

The above steps may take one month or one year—each child progresses at a different rate. Often the determining factor is age.

Q. *My child stutters—how do you help him?*

A. Therapy techniques are different depending on the age of the child and his own reaction to his difficulty with speaking. General goals for therapy are as follows:

1.   The child must develop a trust in the therapist. He must be given the opportunity to relax with the therapist, and to become motivated to change his speaking pattern.

2.   Talk is done about talking. The child needs to realize that everyone has dysfluencies, and that no one's speech is perfect. He has to realize the importance of saying *what* he wants, without worrying about *how* it comes out.

3.   The child's self-image is discussed, and his good qualities and talents are stressed. He needs to realize that his stuttering does not cast a dark shadow over his entire personality.

4.   The child's attitude about listeners' reactions to his speech has to be changed in most cases. He is taught that not everyone is bothered by his stuttering, or made uncomfortable by it. He soon realizes that he himself and a small number of people in his immediate environment are his most critical audience.

5.   With all age groups therapists strive to weaken the strength of the stuttering response. Increasing the amount of fluent speech during therapy, and reducing the amount of stuttering, is essential. Hopefully, his new relaxed attitude about his speech will continue outside the therapy session.

6.   In all cases, any questions a child has about speech and stuttering must be answered (questions such as, "Was I born a stutterer?")

7.   Depending on the age of the child and the severity of the stuttering, the child is asked to pinpoint the situations in which he stutters, with whom it occurs, and on what sounds or words. Then playacting is done in these particular areas. He is made less sensitive to the situations and words that bother him.

8.   Depending on his age, the child is taught ways to control his stuttering; he is shown how to stutter in a more relaxed manner. This leads to his ability to get through the particular situation or word with no stuttering at all.

No two stuttering cases are the same. No *one* method is successful with each child. The above is an outline of some of the things that are discussed and taught in therapy.

Q.   *What is delayed language, and what can be done to help my child who has a language problem?*

A.   Delayed language means that the child does not understand and/or use items of language as do children of his age. Some examples follow.

1.   Receptive language-comprehension of nouns, pronouns, and verbs may be depressed. Instructions given to him may not be understood.

2.   His sentence length may be shorter than that expected.

3.   He may not use plurals, or past or future tenses at an age when he should.

4.   Adjectives and adverbs may not be understood or expressed.

5.   Numbers and colors may not be used or comprehended.

6. Memory for instructions may be poor, causing difficulty in following instructions.

7. The specific words he has in his vocabulary may be immature.

8. He may not understand or express concepts such as size, shape, or texture.

The above are some areas your child may be working on with the speech therapist. Working with a child in language areas entails teaching the particular items with visual, auditory, and tactile aids. For example, to learn plurals a child works with pictures of nouns—actual objects—and he is hearing pluralization throughout the lesson. Language therapy can be done with a child while teaching him a specific sound or while doing fluency therapy, because working on these items requires the use of language.

By Jane Rogers, licensed speech therapist.

Bibliographies

Counselor Bibliography

Adler, Alfred. *The Education of Children*. South Bend, Ind., Gateway Editions, 1978.

Anthony, E.F., and Benedek, T. (eds.). *Parenthood and Psychopathology*. Boston: Little, Brown, 1970.

Arnold, L.E. *Helping Parents Help Their Children*. New York: Brunner-Mazel, 1978.

Bates, Louise Ames, and Ilg, Frances L. *Your Two-Year-Old*. New York: Dell, 1976.

Bowlby, John. *Attachment and Loss*. 2 vols. New York: Basic Books, 1969.

Brandon, Nathaniel. *Honoring the Self*. Boston: Houghton Mifflin, 1983.

Brody, Sylvia. *Patterns of Mothering*. New York: International Universities Press, 1956.

Brody, Sylvia, and Axelrod, Sidney. *Anxiety and Ego Formation in Infancy*. New York: International Universities Press, 1970.

Chinn, P.; Winn, J.; and Walters, R. *Two-Way Talking with Parents of Special Children*. St. Louis: Mosby, 1978.

Chase, Stella, and Thomas, Alexander. *Origins and Evolution of Behavior Disorders*. New York: Brunner-Mazel, 1986.

Coopersmith, Stanley. *Antecedents of Self-Esteem*. San Francisco: H. Freeman, 1967.

Erikson, Erik H. *Childhood and Society*. New York: Norton, 1963.

Freud, Anna. *The Ego and the Mechanisms of Defense*. New York: International University Press, 1936.

Gazda, George M. *Group Counseling: A Developmental Approach*. Boston: Allyn & Bacon, 1971.

Ilg, Frances L. and Ames, Louise A. *Child Behavior*. New York: Harper & Row, 1972.

Inhelder, Barbel, and Piaget, Jean. *The Early Growth of Logic in the Child*. New York: Norton Press and Harper & Row, 1969.

Joseph, Steven M. *Children in Fear*. New York: Holt, Rinehart & Winston, 1974.

Kagan, Jerome. *Infancy: Its Place in Human Development*. New York: Norton, 1978.

Keegan, Robert. *The Evolving Self*. Cambridge, Mass.: Harvard University Press, 1982.

Klaus, Marshall H.; Leger, Treville; and Trause, Mary Anne (eds.). *Maternal Attachment and Mothering Disorders*. Skillman, N.J.: Johnson & Johnson Pediatric Round Table Series, 1987.

Lewis, Jerry; Beeves, Robert; Gosset, John; and Phillip, Virginia. *No Single Thread: Psychological Health in Family Systems*. New York: Harper & Row, 1969.

McCall, Robert. *Infants*. Cambridge, Mass.: Harvard University Press, 1979.

Maier, Henry W. *Three Theories of Child Development*. New York: Harper & Row, 1969.

Masterson, James F. *The Real Self*. New York: Brunner-Mazel, 1985.

Miller, Alice. *Prisoners of Childhood*. New York: Basic Books, 1981.

Minuchin, Salvador, and Fishman, Charles. *Family Therapy Techniques*. Cambridge, Mass.: Harvard University Press, 1981.

Moustakas, Clark. *The Child's Discovery of Himself*. New York: Ballantine Books, 1974.

Mussen, P.; Conger, J.; and Kagan, J. (eds.). *Readings in Child Development*. New York: Harper & Row, 1970.

Muuss, Rolf E. *Theories of Adolescence*. 2d. ed. New York: Random House, 1968.

Parsons, R.A., and Wicks, R. (eds.). *Passive Aggressiveness: Theory and Practice.* New York: Brunner-Mazel, 1984.

Pope, Alice W.; McHale, Susan M.; and Crighead, Edward W. *Self-Esteem Enhancement with Children and Adolescents.* New York: Pergamon Press, 1986.

Redl, Fritz. *When We Deal with Children.* New York: Free Press, 1966.

Redl, Fritz, and Wineman, David. *Controls from Within.* New York: Free Press, 1952.

Reichert, Richard. *Self-Awareness through Group Dynamics.* Dayton, Ohio: George A. Pflaum, 1970.

Sasserman, Valerie J. (ed.). *Minimizing High Risk Parenting.* Skillman, N.J.: Johnson & Johnson Pediatric Round Table Series, 1983.

Scheidlinger, Saul. *Focus on Group Psychotherapy.* New York: International Universities Press, 1982.

Shapiro, David. *Autonomy and Rigid Character.* New York: Basic Books, 1981.

Smith, Sally. *No Easy Answers: The Learning Disabled Child, at Home and at School.* DHEW, 1978. No. (ADM) 77-526, and Des Plaines, Ill.: Bantam Books, 1981.

Sydnor, Granville L.; Akridge, Robert L.; and Parkhill, Nadine L. *Human Relations Training: A Trainer's Manual.* Minden, La.: Human Resources Development Training Institute, 1972.

Watzlawick, Paul; Weakland, John H.; and Fisch, Richard. *Change: Principles of Problem Formation and Problem Resolution.* New York: Norton, 1974.

White, Burton. *The First Three Years of Life.* New York: Avon Books, 1975.

White, Robert W. *Lives in Progress.* New York: Holt, Rinehart & Winston, 1975.

Parents' Bibliography

Preschool Emphasis

Ames, Louise Bates, and Ilg, Frances L. *Your Two-Year-Old*. New York: Delacorte, 1976.
———. *Your Three-Year-Old*. New York: Delacorte, 1976.
———. *Your Four-Year-Old*. New York: Delacorte, 1976.
Boston Women's Health Book Collective. *Ourselves and Our Children*. New York: Random House, 1978.
Brace, Edward R., and Pacanowski, John P. *Childhood Symptoms: Every Parent's Guide to Childhood Illnesses*. New York: Harper & Row, 1980.
Bragg, Joseph. *Children and Adults: Activities for Growing Together*. Englewood Cliffs, N.J.: Prentice-Hall, 1976.
Brazelton, T. Berry. *Doctor and Child*. New York: Delacorte, 1976.
———. *Toddlers and Parents*. New York: Delacorte, 1974.
Briggs, Dorothy C. *Your Child's Self-Esteem*. New York: Doubleday Dolphin, 1985.
Campbell, Ross. *How to Really Love Your Child*. New York: Signet Books, 1977.
Dodson, Fitzhugh. *How to Discipline—With Love*. New York: Rawson, 1977.
Fraiberg, Selma H. *The Magic Years*. New York: Charles Scribner's Sons, 1959.
Gesell, Arnold; Ilg, Frances L.; and Ames, Louise Bates. *Infant and Child in the Culture of Today*. New York: Harper & Row, 1974.
Gordon, Ira. *Baby Learning through Baby Play*. New York: St. Martin's, 1970.
Kaye, Evelyn. *The Family Guide to Children's Television*. New York: Pantheon, 1974.
Kelly, Marguerite, and Parson, Elia. *The Mother's Almanac*. New York: Doubleday, 1975.
Kersey, Katherine. *Sensitive Parenting*. Washington, D.C.: Acropolis Books, Ltd., 1983.
Pulaski, Mary Ann Spencer. *Your Baby's Mind and How It Grows: Piaget's Theory for Parents*. New York: Harper & Row, 1978.
Samuels, Mike, and Samuels, Nancy. *The Well Child Book: Your Child from Four to Twelve*. New York: Simon and Schuster, 1978.
Simon, Sidney, and Olds, Sally W. *Helping Your Child Learn Right from Wrong*. New York: McGraw-Hill, 1977.
Spock, Benjamin, and Rothenberg, Michael. *Dr. Spock's Baby and Child Care*. Dallas, Texas: Hawthorne, 1980.
White, Burton, L. *The First Three Years of Life*. Englewood Cliffs, N.J.; Prentice-Hall, 1975.

Additional Readings for Parents

Baden, Genser, and Levien, Seligsen. *School-Age Child Care*. Dover, Mass.: Auburn House, 1982.
Binswanger, Barbara, and Ryan, Betsy. *Live-In Child Care*. New York: Doubleday Dolphin, 1985.
Committee on Public Education, Group for the Advancement of Psychiatry. *The Joys and Sorrows of Parenthood*. New York: Scribner's, 1973.

Dodson, Fitzhugh, *How to Parent.* Los Angeles, Calif.: Nash Publishing Co., 1970.
Fraiberg, Selma. H. *Every Child's Birthright: In Defense of Mothering.* New York: Basic Books, 1977.
Gardner, Richard A. *Understanding Children.* New York: Aronson, 1973.
Granger, R.H. *Your Child from One to Six.* Washington, D.C.: DHEW. DHEW Pub. No. (OHOS) 77-30026, 1977.
Kappelman, Murray. *Raising the Only Child.* New York: Dutton, 1975.
Missildine, W. *Your Inner Child of the Past.* New York: Simon and Schuster, 1963.
Patterson, G.R., and Gullion, M.E. *Living with Children: New Methods for Parents and Teachers.* Champaign, Ill.: Research Press, 1968.
Scarr, Sandra. *Mother Care—Other Care.* New York: Basic Books, 1980.

For Parents of Adolescents

Bush, Richard. *When a Child Needs Help: A Parents' Guide to Child Therapy.* Boston: Dell, 1980.
Ginnot, H. *Between Parent and Teenager.* New York: Avon, 1971.
Muuss, R.E., *Theories of Adolescence.* 2d ed. New York: Random House, 1968.
Oettinger, K.B. *Normal Adolescence.* New York: Scribner's, 1968.
Stone, J., and Church, J. *Childhood and Adolescence.* New York: Random House, 1975.

For Single Parents

Understanding and Coping with Separation and Divorce

Hunt, Morton. *The World of the Formerly Married.* New York: McGraw-Hill, 1966.
Krantzler, M. *Creative Divorce.* New York: New American Library, 1973.
Weiss, Robert S. *Marital Separation.* New York: Basic Books, 1975.

Of Particular Interest to Men

Atkin, Edith. *Part-Time Father.* New York: Vanguard Press, 1976.
Epstein, Joseph. *Divorce in America.* New York: Dutton, 1974.

Of Particular Interest to Women

Bequaert, Lucia H. *Single Women: Alone and Together.* Boston: Beacon Press, 1976.
Women in Transition, Inc. *Women in Transition: A Feminist Handbook on Separation and Divorce.* New York: Scribner's, 1975.

The Effects of Divorce on Children and Their Relationships

Goldstein, J.; Freud, A.; and Solnit, A. *Beyond the Best Interest of the Child.* Monroe, La.: Free Press, 1973.
Grollman, Earl A. *Explaining Divorce to Children.* Boston: Beacon Press, 1969.
Krantzler, M. *Creative Divorce.* New York: New American Library, 1973.
Steinzor, Bernard. *When Parents Divorce.* New York: Pantheon, 1969.
Stuart, Irving, and Abt, Lawrence. *Children of Separation and Divorce.* New York: Grossman, 1972.
Weiss, Robert S. *Marital Separation.* New York: Basic Books, 1975.

To Be Read to Children

Gardner, Richard A. *The Boys and Girls Book about Divorce.* New York: Bantam Books, 1971.
Grollman, Earl A. *Explaining Divorce to Children.* Boston: Beacon Press, 1969.

Of General Interest in Understanding and Coping with Children

Buxbaum, Edith. *Your Child Makes Sense.* New York: International Universities Press, 1949.

Fraiberg, Selma. *The Magic Years.* New York: Scribner's, 1959.

Ginott, Haim. *Between Parent and Child.* New York: Avon, 1965.

Gordon, Thomas. *Parent Effectiveness Training.* New York: New American Library, 1975.

Salk, Lee. *What Every Child Would Like His Parents to Know.* New York: Warner Paperback Library, 1972.

For Parents of Children with Special Needs

Brutten, M.; Richardson, S.; and Mangel, C. *Something's Wrong with My Child.* San Diego, Calif.: Harcourt, Brace, Jovanovich, 1973.

Clay, M. *The Early Detection of Reading Difficulties.* Portsmouth, N.H.: Heinemann Pub. Co., 1979.

Crosby, R.M.N. *The Waysiders.* New York: Delacorte Press, 1968.

Mason, J. *Pre-Reading: A Developmental Perspective.* Technical Report No. 198. Urbana, Ill.: University of Illinois, 1981.

Moore, C.B., and Morton, K.G. *A Reader's Guide for Parents of Children with Mental, Physical, or Emotional Disabilities.* Rockville, Md.; DHEW. DHEW Pub. No. (HSA) 77-5290, 1977.

Perk, C., and Shapiro, L. *You Are Not Alone.* Boston: Little, Brown, 1976.

Puske, R. *New Directions for Parents of Persons Who Are Retarded.* Nashville, Tenn.: Abingdon Press, 1973.

Sapin, G. Selma; Nitzburg, Ann C. *Children with Learning Problems.* New York: Bruner/Mazel, Inc., 1978.

Smith, Sally L. *No Easy Answers: The Learning Disabled Child.* Des Plaines, Ill.: Bantam Books, 1981.

Index

About the Author

Dr. Frieda A. Lang—wife, mother, teacher, counselor, and psychologist—has had a wide range of experience. She is a three-time graduate of Boston University, and she has worked as a college and secondary school teacher, high school counselor, and psychologist. At present she is a psychotherapist in private practice.

Acting on the premise that most children's learning and social-emotional adjustment problems can be successfully mitigated through counseling and guiding parents in groups, she developed a successful and easy to implement program for use by other professionals. This book presents her rationale, a step-by-step program that is given during two-hour sessions over a period of fifteen weeks and contains a pre- and post-evaluation for both parents and group leaders.